FORM

CRITICISM

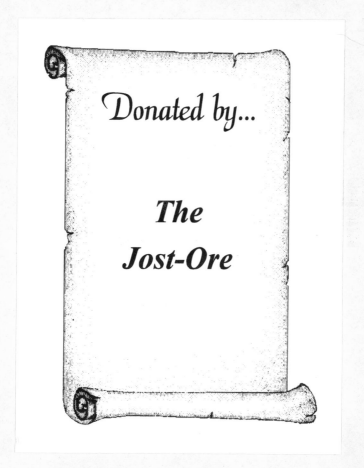

Harper Torchbooks
The Academy Library
Harper & Brothers
New York

FORM CRITICISM

TWO ESSAYS ON NEW TESTAMENT RESEARCH

The Study of the Synoptic Gospels

by RUDOLPH BULTMANN

Primitive Christianity in the Light of Gospel Research

by KARL KUNDSIN

Translated by FREDERICK C. GRANT

CONTENTS

PART ONE

THE STUDY OF THE SYNOPTIC GOSPELS
By RUDOLF BULTMANN

PART TWO

PRIMITIVE CHRISTIANITY IN THE
LIGHT OF GOSPEL RESEARCH
By KARL KUNDSIN

CONTENTS

PREFACE TO THE TORCHBOOK EDITION

For over forty years now, students of the New Testament have been aware of the existence of a school of gospel research known as Form Criticism—or, more accurately, *Formgeschichte*, Form History. Its attention has been devoted to the component units into which the tradition underlying the Synoptic Gospels may be analyzed. It endeavors to study the oral tradition at a stage prior to its crystallization in gospels, or even in sources underlying the gospels, whether written documents or cycles of fixed tradition—such as Q, the pre-Marcan outline of Jesus' ministry, the sequences in the narratives and discourse material, the Passion Narrative, and so on. A comparison of other processes of development in oral tradition, chiefly oriental, and the evidence of editorial modification or elaboration within the gospels themselves, both suggest the probability that some kind of orderly procedure, determined in part by folk psychology, may be traced in this earlier period. There are, it is assumed, certain positive principles controlling the development of tradition; the present task of the New Testament critic, now that the Synoptic sources are fairly generally recognized, is to examine the operation of these principles during the relatively brief period between the death of Jesus and the earliest written accounts of his life and teaching. Thus Form Criticism may be looked upon as a necessary step in research; if successful, it may lead us back to the fountain-head of Christian origins. A method of such promise deserves the most thorough examination by everyone interested in the study of the gospels, whether from the literary, the historical, or the purely religious point of view.

Form Criticism began during, or even before, World War I. We find anticipations of it in the work of such earlier scholars as Johannes Weiss and Julius Wellhausen—and above all in the work of Hermann Gunkel, who applied the theory to the history and legends in the Old Testament. But its full application came only with the work of Rudolf Bultmann and Martin Dibelius. The two major works of these leaders in the movement are still of fundamental importance for every student of Form Criticism. Rudolf Bultmann's *History of the Synoptic Tradition* (*Die Geschichte der synoptischen Tradition*, 2d ed., Göttingen, 1931) has now been translated into English by John Marsh; Martin Dibelius's *From Tradition to Gospel* (a translation of the second edition of *Die Formgeschichte des Evangeliums,* New York, 1935) has long been out of print and improcurable. Among the earliest English works, dealing with the new school and its method, were *The Gospel before the Gospels* by Burton Scott Easton (New York, 1928) and *The Formation of the Gospel Tradition* by Vincent Taylor (London, 1933). These books helped to make clear the immense importance of the movement, and its potential contribution to our knowledge of early church history, the origin of the New Testament and especially the gospels, and the life and teaching of Jesus. The present volume originated at about that same time when, for the sake of my students, I translated the two essays by Bultmann and Kundsin contained herein—the American publishers combined the two into one book. For the past twenty-five years it has provided a useful introduction to the subject for many students, here and abroad, and one hopes it will continue to do so in this new format.

During the long quarter century since the translation appeared, the study of the gospels has progressed steadily (if not spectacularly) here, in Great Britain, and on the Continent—in spite of the irreparable setback to all learning (except scientific) caused by the Second World War, its antecedents, preliminaries, and ghastly aftermath. The central principle of Form Criticism has been fully established, viz. that the earliest gospel traditions circulated orally within the church, whose religious needs they served, and were only gradually gathered together into groups, blocs, or sequences —and finally gospels. These traditions were by no means the literary creation of imaginative writers in search of a reading public. In many cases it is quite possible to distinguish the original "form" of these traditions from their later modification, editorial revision, and resetting given them by the evangelists—and this is what Form Criticism consists in, viz. the restoration of the gospel traditions to their original form.[1] Form Criticism is not a revolutionary method designed to do away with literary and historical criticism, or to provide a short-cut, open to all comers, which will excuse them from the toil of patient philological analysis, textual criticism, comparative study of parallel passages, and the whole involved task of exegesis.

[1] See the reconstruction in Martin Dibelius's little book, *Die Botschaft von Jesus Christus,* which I translated under the title, *The Message of Jesus Christ: the Tradition of the Early Christian Communities,* New York, 1939.

It is only one more tool, and a most valuable one when
wielded by experts, especially by such gifted inter-
preters as Rudolf Bultmann and the late Martin
Dibelius. Its results are clearly evident and appreciable
by all readers of the New Testament. The figure of
Jesus, his character, and the positive content of his
teaching, his proclamation of the approaching Kingdom of God, the course of his brief career in Galilee
and Jerusalem, the impact which he made upon his
contemporaries, the beginnings of the Christian movement and the origin of the Christian church—all this
is far more certainly delimited and more accurately
understood as a result of the past forty years of Form
Criticism, the influence of which has extended, as Dr.
Bultmann points out in his Note, far beyond the ranks
of the form critics.[2] The change is reflected, e.g., in the
new edition of my *Growth of the Gospels* (1933), now
entirely rewritten and considerably enlarged (including
a bibliography, pp. 203–207), under the title *The
Gospels, Their Origin and Their Growth* (New York,
Harper, 1957; London, Faber, 1959). But this is only
one book among several which show the new orientation in New Testament study, and attest the value of
the work of the school's "founding fathers," Rudolf
Bultmann and Martin Dibelius.

F. C. C.

New York
January 1962

---

[2] See the two beautiful, moving, constructive portrayals of the life
of Jesus in Martin Dibelius's *Jesus* (Philadelphia, 1949) and Günther
Bornkamm's *Jesus von Nazareth* (New York, 1960). Both works take
Form Criticism for granted and use it throughout.

NOTE TO THE TORCHBOOK EDITION

By RUDOLF BULTMANN

The purpose of Form Criticism is to study the history of the oral tradition behind the gospels.[1] This method of research has proved fruitful in the exposition of the Synoptic Gospels and in the investigation of the earliest beginnings of Christianity. Aside from Form Criticism, efforts have continued, by means of literary analysis, to prove the existence of written sources for the Synoptics. And there has been no lack of opponents of the new method; yet this has been only a relative opposition, as in the work of Wilfred L. Knox, *The Sources of the Synoptic Gospels* (two vols., Cambridge Univ. Press, 1953, 1957). Even though Knox was opposed to Form Criticism, he nevertheless could not avoid making use of form-critical observations in his own analysis. The relation between the two methods is set forth by Kendrick Grobel in his book, *Formgeschichte und synoptische Quellenanalyse* (Göttingen, 1937).

This is not the place for an account of the form-critical works that have appeared since 1934, when the present work first made its appearance in English. A full account is given by Gerhard Iber in the *Theologische Rundschau, N. F.* 24, 1957-58. In addition to the works of Burton Scott Easton (*The Gospel Before the Gospels,* 1928) and Vincent Taylor (*The Forma-*

---

[1] For the moment I am disregarding the fact that Form Criticism has also been applied to other New Testament writings than the gospels. For an account of this further extension of the method, see Martin Dibelius's article in the *Theologische Rundschau,* 1931, pp. 207–242.

tion of the Gospel Tradition, 1933), I would refer to
the volume by Frederick C. Grant, *The Earliest Gospel*
(New York, 1943) and the article by C. H. Dodd,
"The Framework of the Gospel Narrative," in the *Ex-
pository Times* (1932, reprinted in his *New Testament
Studies,* London, 1952; New York, 1954). A whole
series of special studies in Form Criticism by Martin
Dibelius has been gathered together in his posthumous
work, *Botschaft und Geschichte* (two vols., Tübingen,
1952, 1953). For the form-critical study of the gospel
parables, the two volumes by C. H. Dodd, *The Parables
of the Kingdom* (10th ed., New York, 1950), and
Joachim Jeremias, *The Parables of Jesus* (4th ed., 1956;
Eng. tr. of the 3d ed., New York, 1955), are especially
important.

A few additions should be made to the present volume. First, on the literature dealing with the trial of
Jesus, in Note 1 to Chapter VII (p. 75) see also the
titles given in the *Ergänzungsheft* to my *Geschichte der
synoptischen Tradition* (Göttingen, 1958, p. 40) and
in the new English translation of the *History.* Secondly,
in connection with Chapter II, I would like to point
out that the hypothesis of Jewish Gnosticism has since
been proved by the discovery of manuscripts in the
caves near the Dead Sea—the so-called "Dead Sea
Scrolls." The best account of these manuscripts is the
book by Millar Burrows, *The Dead Sea Scrolls* (New
York, 1955), which also gives a translation of the more
important texts. (See also his supplementary volume,
More Light on the Dead Sea Scrolls, New York, 1958.)
These manuscripts come from some Jewish sect, presumably the Essenes. In many of them is found the

typical Gnostic dualism of Light and Darkness, a type of thought which originated in Iran. This is no highly developed type of Gnosis, since it lacks the Gnostic Redeemer mythology—at least none is apparent in the documents thus far discovered and published. But the chief matter of interest is the fact that here was a community, whose character is reflected in the manuscripts, which provided an analogy to the early Christian. Both groups viewed themselves as the eschatological community and were awaiting the End of the Age, the coming Judgment and salvation. The view which is occasionally set forth, that Jesus and his disciples came from this heretical Jewish community, cannot be maintained. A few parallels in detail indicate a certain relationship, but by no means prove the dependence of Jesus and his followers upon the other group. Jesus' preaching differs radically from the teaching of the Qumran sect, for he broke with Jewish legalism—and extreme legalism was characteristic of the sect. On the relation of Jesus and the synoptic tradition to the teaching of the Qumran sect, with reference to the Jewish Law, see Herbert Braun's work, *Spätjüdisch-häretischer und frühchristlichen Radikalismus* (two vols., Tübingen, 1957). And on the significance of the Dead Sea Scrolls for the New Testament as a whole, see the essays, by various authors, in Krister Stendahl's *The Scrolls and the New Testament* (New York, 1957).

The soundness of Form Criticism has been demonstrated in recent years, since it has served, and still continues to serve, as the presupposition of further research. Form Criticism begins with the realization that the tradition contained in the Synoptic Gospels originally consisted of separate units, which were joined together editorially by the evangelists. Form Criticism is therefore concerned to distinguish these units of tradition, and to discover their earliest form and origin in the life of the early Christian community (see Chapter III). It views the gospels as essentially compilations of this older material. But it also studies them as finished works, in order to evaluate the literary activity of the evangelists, and to discover the theological motives that guided them. This phase of the subject certainly has not been entirely overlooked, as is shown by the works of Wilhelm Wrede, Frederick Grant, and C. H. Dodd. But it is now the center of interest. This study began with the following writings: For Mark: W. Marxsen, *Der Evangelist Markus* (Göttingen, 1956); for Matthew: Krister Stendahl, *The School of St. Matthew* (Uppsala, 1954); N. A. Dahl, "Die Passionsgeschichte bei Matthäus," in the journal *New Testament Studies* (Vol. II, 1955-56, pp. 17-32); and Günther Bornkamm, "Enderwartung und Kirche im Matthäusevangelium," in *The Background of the New Testament and its Eschatology* (the *Festschrift* in honor of C. H. Dodd, Cambridge, 1956, pp. 222-260); for Luke: H. Conzelmann, *Die Mitte der Zeit* (Tübingen, 1954). If one ought to say that works like these go a step beyond Form Criticism, it nevertheless remains true that they are at the same time a confirmation of it, since they presuppose its method and contribution.

Marburg, Germany
January, 1962

PART ONE

THE STUDY OF THE SYNOPTIC GOSPELS

By Rudolf Bultmann

FOREWORD

Professor Bultmann's little work, now presented in English translation, appeared in Germany under the title, *Die Erforschung der Synoptischen Evangelien* (second, enlarged and improved edition, 1930), as the first volume in the New Testament section of the series already named. It is a 'popular' exposition of the method elaborated at far greater length, and all but exhaustively, in his *History of the Synoptic Tradition* (*Geschichte der Synoptischen Tradition*, 2d ed., 1931), to which the reader familiar with German may wish to turn after reading the present briefer, introductory volume. Another important work of the Marburg professor is *Jesus,* the first volume in a series of popular biographical sketches entitled *The Immortals* (*Die Unsterblichen*), in which, passing on from the details of the literary criticism of the gospels, the author undertakes to reconstruct the life and teaching of our Lord on the basis of the data thus arrived at. It is in this last named work chiefly that Professor Bultmann's sympathies with the Barthian school of theology are most conspicuous.

Another form critic has referred to Professor Bultmann's 'iron scepticism.'[1] And it may be that the American and British reader will be similarly impressed. But for our purpose, viz., to grasp the main outlines of the form-historical method, and to study its

tendency and chief results, it is worth while to examine
the method in its clearest and most extreme form.
There is little doubt that the coming generation of New
Testament scholarship will devote an increasing
amount of attention to this method and its results. To
close our eyes and refuse to consider the problems it
raises would be fatal, and is really impossible except
upon an out-and-out Fundamentalist view of Holy
Scripture. But such a procedure is as unnecessary as it
is blind and unseeing. There are substantial gains to
be derived from the study — not least, as I have tried
to show in my *Growth of the Gospels,*[2] a new conception of the vitality of the earliest ecclesiastical tradition
and its close relation to the religious and social situation in which the first believers found themselves, and
to the needs and aspirations, the hopes and aims of the
early church. Form criticism helps us to understand
more sympathetically the problems with which the
'teachers' of the New Testament period were confronted, and their methods as they went about their task.
Form criticism gives us a renewed sense of the great-
ness, and the essential trustworthiness, of the earliest
evangelical tradition; and it enables us to distinguish, in
that tradition, 'the living and abiding voice' of one
who 'spake as never man spake' and who yet spake
'as man.' It is his authentic voice we would fain hear,
in these days, not the mere echo of his words upon the
lips even of the holiest and most devoted of his disciples — even though it be true that the echo often
brings us a word we can by no means afford to dis-

regard. After all, it is Jesus himself we would see and hear; and though it seems certain we shall never be able to write his full biography, what we do have of his teaching is infinitely precious —

> 'This is all ye know . . .
> And all ye need to know.'

For the words of Jesus, as an early second-century writer truly described them, 'are spirit and . . . life' (John vi. 63). It is the promise of Form criticism that it will give us a better understanding of Jesus' own authentic words, as well as a clearer test for distinguishing his own veritable utterances from later accretions and interpretations, added in the course of handing down the tradition. A method offering such a promise deserves the most careful consideration.

F. C. G.

CHAPTER I

THE PROBLEMS AND SOLUTIONS OF EARLIER RESEARCH

The special interest which attaches to the Synoptic Gospels is explained by the fact that they are our most important sources for the historical life and work of Jesus of Nazareth. There used to be a time, and for readers without historical education and interests the condition still remains, in which the juxtaposition of the three Gospels of Matthew, Mark and Luke occasioned no difficult problem; the three narratives (and to them was added that of John) were simply put side by side, and harmonized one with another, with the result that a picture of the life of Jesus was produced. As soon, however, as modern historical interest became awakened, this juxtaposition of the three Synoptics, with their peculiar agreements and differences, provided a certain difficulty. In the first place, the agreements indicated that some kind of literary relationship must exist between the three. How was this to be thought of? As the use by one evangelist of the work of one of the others? Or did one of them make use of the other two, or did two of them make use of the third? And which of them is the user, which the used? All these various possibilities have been examined in the course of research since the period of Rationalism, not to mention earlier attempts, which took place now and then in the ancient and medieval church. There are, of course, other possibilities: may not the agreements go back to some lost primitive gospel which the three Synoptists used? Or if not to a complete gospel, at least to single fragments or written sketches of the works and words of Jesus? Or may not the oral tradition of the Christian church have arrived at a sufficiently fixed form, so that the evangelists needed only to draw from this source? Moreover, in the next place, how are the differences to be accounted for — the fact, for example, that the evangelists recount the same events and sayings in different form, and that one will tell more, the other less? Is the explanation to be found in the fact that their sources were in disagreement, that one gave a richer and more exact narration than another; or are they themselves responsible in that they altered the evangelic material from their own point of view and to suit the definite conditions of their own time and situation? How, for example, is the wealth of material which Matthew and Luke have in contrast to Mark to be explained, and likewise the narratives which each of them has in excess of the other? Were good early narratives still available, or were the new narratives and words the products of imagination? These possibilities have likewise often been put forward; and just as in the answer to the first question, so also these possibilities contain in them a certain amount of truth which no one can determine by a simple 'either — or'; rather is it evident that the history of the origin of the Synoptic Gospels is very complicated.

As a result of the labors of successive generations since the end of the eighteenth century, New Testament research has arrived at certain results which appear to be sufficiently assured to be taken for granted, and which in their general outlines are quite simple. Quite generally recognized is the so-called Two Source Theory, that is, the hypothesis that Mark is the oldest gospel and was used by Matthew and Luke. These two evangelists made use, in addition to Mark, of a lost source which was a collection of the sayings of Jesus, which they worked into the text of Mark in quite different ways. If one wishes to test this conclusion, he should use a Synopsis (or Harmony of the Gospels), that is, a book in which the texts of the three evangelists are printed side by side.[1] In the comparison of passages one must take into account the quantity of material as well as its detailed formulation. Most weight, however, falls upon the order, and one really cannot escape the conclusion if this is examined carefully. The fact becomes almost obvious that the Gospel of Mark underlies the outline of the other two. Moreover, if one removes the text of Mark, so to speak, from Matthew and Luke, there still remains a fairly large number of passages in close agreement, containing for the most part words and sayings of Jesus, whose common agreements are best explained by the supposition that they originated in a collection of sayings which was used by both Matthew and Luke.

But a number of problems still remain. It is, for example, probable that the text of Mark which the two

other evangelists used lay before them in an older form
than that in which we have it today. This *Urmarcus*
(as it is usually called) was altered and enlarged at
certain points; but it can scarcely be distinguished from
the present text of Mark in any important way. So
too the question remains an open one, regarding the
sources of Mark: whether the tradition he collected was
oral or already in written form, or whether indeed he
made use of collections of written material which were
already in existence. Whether Mark or the Sayings-
document is the older or more reliable, whether or not
Mark already knew the collection of sayings and perhaps made occasional use of it, cannot be answered
with assurance; but it is probable that the collection of
sayings, like the Gospel of Mark itself, had not yet arrived at a fixed and final form, but was being enlarged
here and there, and did not lie before Matthew and
Luke in quite the same shape. It is extremely unlikely
that Luke knew or made use of Matthew or vice versa.
Whence Matthew and Luke derived their material, outside Mark and the collection of sayings, we cannot say.
The English scholar B. H. Streeter, in a recent work of
great acumen (*The Four Gospels,* 1924), has under-
taken to show that Matthew and Luke each used a
special source in addition to Mark and the Sayings.
Accordingly, we must now speak of a 'Four Source
Hypothesis' as well as a 'Two Source Hypothesis.'
However, all such attempted solutions are quite uncertain. In any case we may say that the age and the historical value of this peculiar matter are quite diverse.

The date of the gospels cannot be accurately determined. It appears as a result of investigation of the language that the material in the Sayings collection, and in large measure that of Mark as well, goes back to Aramaic tradition, and was therefore originally formulated in the language which Jesus and his disciples spoke. It is, moreover, probable that the collection of sayings was originally made in Aramaic and then translated into Greek — perhaps more than once — and so reached the evangelists Matthew and Luke. But it is certain that the Gospel of Mark as a whole is no translation out of Aramaic but was originally written in Greek; whether this was before the destruction of Jerusalem in the year 70 or soon after, it is impossible to say. At any rate, it was not the work of a disciple of Jesus or of a member of the primitive community; and the same is true of Matthew and Luke. Like Mark, they originated in Greek Christianity, of course with the difference that Matthew was a Greek-Jewish Christian, Luke a Gentile Christian — at any rate according to all probabilities. The composition of the Gospels of Matthew and Luke may be placed in the period from 70 to 100 A.D., probably nearer 100 than 70. We know from St. Paul (especially from the Epistle to the Galatians) that the Gentile Mission provided a grave problem for the primitive community, and that at first the Gentile Christians were expected to observe the Jewish Law. For Matthew and Luke, however, it is (as for Mark) already self-evident that the gospel, and the gospel alone apart from the Law, was meant for the heathen.

Where, as in Matthew, a different view appears (e.g.
x. 5–6; xv. 24), it is not the evangelist but the material he
uses that is responsible; his own point of view receives
expression, for example, in xxviii. 19. Corresponding
to this is Luke xxiv. 47. On the other hand, none of
the Synoptists betrays any influence of the ecclesiastical
problems and controversies that were characteristic of
the second century.

CHAPTER II

THE NEW RELIGIOUS AND LITERARY-HISTORICAL INQUIRIES

One may justly maintain that what has been set forth hitherto represents the assured results of research. Now, however, begin those most interesting and most difficult questions with which the research of the present day is engaged. One may point out two characteristics of contemporary research. The first is the new religious-historical point of view. The researches of Bousset and Heitmüller have made clear the meaning of the transition of the Christian evangel from Palestinian-Jewish to Hellenistic territory, and the enormous distinction which existed between Palestinian and Hellenistic Christianity (see especially Bousset's great work *Kyrios Christos,* 2d ed., 1921). The contrast is clear, first of all, in that for the Palestinian-Jewish Christians Jesus was the Messiah, whose return as the Son of Man they ardently expected; while for the Hellenistic-Gentile Christians Jesus was primarily the Lord whom they worshipped in their common cult (i.e. in divine worship),.whose presence they experienced in the activities of the Spirit. Even though these believers were also under the influence of the 'eschatological' tension (that is, they expected the immediate end of the world and the arrival of the Kingdom of God and the Reign

of the Messiah), it was the present exalted Lord who
stood in their midst; their piety was nourished by contemporary experiences, which were roused by the mys-
teries of their solemn worship, and they even rose to the
heights of genuine mysticism. To the question, if and
how these two types of primitive Christianity still
formed a unity, we can at this point only suggest the
answer. Each group understood salvation to be an
' other-worldly ' life received as a gift from God, in comparison with which all the good things of this world
fade away, a life that brought with it forgiveness of
sins, and obligated one to a new kind of conduct. It
is the same salvation, which is by one group shared inwardly in expectation of participating in the great
events of the End, already felt to be under way, and of
which the other group became certain in the solemnity
of public worship. The important thing is that for
either group one was assured of salvation through that
which God had accomplished in the person and work
of Jesus. Aside from this general agreement, however,
there existed great differences, and since our gospels
arose out of Greek Christianity, the distinction provides
us with a criterion which frequently enables us to determine whether this or that feature belongs to the older
tradition or was composed later.

However, the distinction between Palestinian and
Hellenistic Christianity does not exhaust the possibilities. The latest discoveries and researches have
clearly suggested the question, whether or not we must
distinguish even in Palestinian Christianity two dif-

ferent levels, one of which enjoyed from the outset a close relation with Hellenistic piety. For some time now, New Testament research has recognized that certain circles of Palestinian Judaism were influenced by Oriental speculations regarding the origin and end of the world, concerning the nature of man and his redemption, speculations similar to those which we find in later Christian Gnosticism. Recent works, especially those of the philologist Reitzenstein, have made clearer the character of this Jewish ' Gnosis,' its mythology and its piety. Much stronger than has hitherto been supposed was the influence, in apocalyptic Jewish circles, of the Iranian-Babylonian religion of redemption, with its mythological speculations and its own peculiar rites. This type of piety manifested itself, in the period around the beginning of the Christian era, in a multitude of tiny sects which practiced a variety of rites, chiefly baptism, and plumbed the depths of apocalyptic fantasy. Within Judaism itself one such sect was that of the Essenes, concerning which, however, we have very little reliable information. In all probability John the Baptist and his sect belonged in this classification. And it is at least possible that Jesus, who according to the narrative of the Synoptists was baptized by John, and his earliest followers as well, originally stood in much closer contact with this ' Baptist ' type of Judaism, subject as it was to strong Oriental influence; and that the movement originated by Jesus separated itself from the Baptist sect to which it had originally belonged and gradually moved in the direction of normal Judaism, for which the religion of the Law and the problem of its fulfilment were central. The Synoptic Gospels present us with both phases: not only with a certain agreement between the Baptist sect and Jesus (Matt. xi. 7–11a; xi. 16–19; xxi. 32), but also with a certain rivalry between the two (Mark ii. 28; Matt. xi. 11b; Luke xi. 1b); and that the controversy between the disciples of John and those of Jesus continued for some time is clear from John i. 6–8, 15, 19–34; iii. 22–30; Acts xix. 1–7. It is therefore possible that the picture which the Synoptists give us of the person and the message of Jesus has obliterated many an older trait, and that many a word is attributed to him which he did not utter. It is also possible that the eschatological message of the coming Son of Man played a much larger part in the preaching of Jesus and the question of the Law a much less important one than is now represented in the Synoptic tradition. We are dealing only with possibilities, with questions which have only recently emerged for research and which must engage its attention for some time to come. It is therefore impossible to say at present to what results they will lead. One can only emphasize the uncertainty of our knowledge of the person and work of the historical Jesus and likewise of the origin of Christianity.

The second feature of contemporary Gospel research is the new literary-historical method of approach which has come to be known as Form criticism. As we have noted, research had already arrived at the result that the

Gospel of Mark was the oldest of the three Synoptics, and that by its side was to be found the collection of Sayings as another old source. It was assumed in the generation of such experts as H. J. Holtzmann, A. Jülicher, and J. Weiss that one could make out from Mark and Q (the Sayings-document) the course of the life of Jesus and the content of his preaching with relative certainty. The inner development of the life of Jesus was inferred from the development of his Messianic consciousness: that is, from his steadily advancing claim to Messiahship, of which he was not entirely certain at the beginning and accordingly kept secret, and which he publicly acknowledged only at the end of his life; which consciousness as it gradually ripened in himself he permitted gradually to ripen likewise in his disciples. The outward development of his life, on the other hand, was characterized by an initial success and then by a gradual desertion on the part of the people, whose hopes he had disappointed, and most of all by the opposition of the scribes and Pharisees. The chief content of the preaching of Jesus was his message of the Kingdom of God, which was neither a purely spiritual state nor a society of the pious realizing itself historically in the midst of this world, but was the heavenly Kingdom expected to come miraculously and catastrophically in the immediate future. These scholars scarcely recognized the problem, viz., how the moral demands of Jesus were related to this ' eschatological ' message — the former receiving expression in many of his sayings (e.g. Matt. v. 20-45; vi. 1-34) and in the controversies with the scribes, and containing practically no traces of the eschatological expectation.

On the other hand, W. Wrede had already demonstrated in his book *The Messianic Secret in the Gospels* (*Das Messiasgeheimnis in den Evangelien,* 1901), undoubtedly the most important work in the field of gospel research in the generation now past, that although Mark is indeed the oldest gospel, its narrative cannot be accepted as an exact account of the history of Jesus; that Mark is really dominated by the theology of the Church and by a dogmatic conception of Christ; and that he arranged and revised the old traditional material out of which his gospel is composed in accordance with his own ideas, so that one cannot make out from his narrative either the development of the Messianic consciousness and claim of Jesus or the course of his activity, nor the reasons for his failure and death. Wellhausen in his Commentaries on the Gospels (1905 and following) reinforced and demonstrated essentially the same conclusion: in each of the gospels one must distinguish between the old tradition and the redactional contribution of the evangelist; the former consists essentially in single brief units; the latter not only altered many of the details but first gave its continuity to the whole, thus creating the artificial effect of a historical development. Especially important is Wellhausen's demonstration that the Sayings-document, like Mark, has been influenced by the theology of the primitive church: it grew out of the primitive community and is steeped in its views and interests, and therefore gives us no infallible reflection of the preaching of Jesus.

The result of these works was at once a widespread
but perfectly futile discussion of the Messianic consciousness of Jesus. To what extent had Jesus looked
upon himself as Messiah in the Jewish sense, to what
extent did he transform the Jewish Messianic conception? Did he look upon himself as Messiah from the
very beginning — say from the time of his baptism —
or did his Messianic consciousness grow gradually, first
developing, perhaps, toward the end of his ministry?
Was the Messianic consciousness for him a matter of
pride and of consolation in the midst of opposition, or
was it a burden hard to bear? Was it essential or was
it a relatively indifferent form of his sense of vocation?
Indeed, did he hold himself to be the Messiah at all, or
was this the product of the faith of his followers?
These were the typical questions, and all of these tan-
talizing possibilities were investigated by individual
scholars and variously affirmed and denied; one can
scarcely gain a stronger impression of the uncertainty
of our knowledge concerning the person of Jesus than
by putting together what the various investigators of
the Messianic consciousness of Jesus have thought. It
is noteworthy that little attention has been given to the
outward course of the life of Jesus and the grounds of
his condemnation. The assurance with which formerly
it was assumed that the ministry of Jesus was limited to
one year has indeed weakened since it has come to be
recognized that the outline of Mark is not historical.
But what were the actual external factors determining
his fate, and what it was that led him to the cross —
these questions are scarcely asked, as if it were self-

evident that the enmity of the scribes and Pharisees
compassed his death. The problem, how the eschatological and the ethical teaching of Jesus are related one
to the other, has come at last to be recognized. It is in
truth far from easy to say how an eschatological prophet
who sees the end of the world approaching, who senses
the arrival of the Kingdom of God, and accordingly
pronounces blessed those of his contemporaries who are
prepared for it (Matt. xiii. 16–17; v. 3–9; xi. 5–6 etc.) —
to say how such a person could argue over questions of
the Law and turn off epigrammatic proverbs like a
Jewish rabbi (since to practically all the moral directions of Jesus there are parallel and related words of
Jewish rabbis), in words which contain simply no hint
of eschatological tension (e.g. Matt. vi. 19–21, 25–34; vii.
1, 2, 7; x. 29; Luke xiv. 7–11; Mark ii. 27; iv. 21). Wellhausen looked upon the ethical teaching as the genuine
historical nucleus, and believed that the eschatological
sayings were for the most part the products of the primitive Christian community, which after Jesus' death was
strongly influenced by the Messianic expectations.
Others, like J. Weiss and A. Schweitzer, held, contrari-
wise, the eschatological preaching to be the characteristic message of the historical Jesus, and either ignored
the moral directions or explained them as 'interim
ethic,' that is, as requirements which lacked general
validity but which held good for this last brief space of
time which was to precede the end.

CHAPTER III

THE DISTINCTION BETWEEN THE TRADI-
TIONAL MATERIAL AND ITS REDAC-
TION: FORM CRITICISM

Where is the way leading out of such perplexities?
It is certainly not sufficient to pass judgment in each individual case upon the authenticity of a saying or narrative of Jesus in accordance with one's own impressions;
instead, one must endeavor to judge in accordance with
a systematic investigation of the strata or strands of
tradition the gospels contain. One must look for clues
leading back behind the oldest attainable sources, the
Gospel of Mark and the Sayings-source reconstructed
out of Matthew and Luke, and try to understand the
historical process by which they came into existence.
The first step is to distinguish between the traditional
material which the evangelists used and their editorial
additions. This task, which Wellhausen recognized,
was systematically carried through by K. L. Schmidt
(*Der Rahmen der Geschichte Jesu,* i.e. *The Framework
of the History of Jesus,* 1919). It may be seen quite
clearly that the original tradition was made up almost
entirely of brief single units (sayings or short narratives), and that almost all references to time and place
which serve to connect up the single sections into a
larger context are the editorial work of the evangelists.

These make use of typical formulas of transition which are spread, so to speak, over an apparently limited body of local tradition in order to provide the background of the particular scenes and the framework of the life of Jesus as a whole: the house, the road, the mountain, the shore; situations such as Jesus in the boat, upon a journey, as a guest at a meal, or in the synagogue at public worship. Entirely schematic is the appearance of the crowds, the opponents, and the attending disciples. In my book (*The History of the Synoptic Tradition, Die Geschichte der Synoptischen Tradition,* 1921; second edition, 1931, pp. 347–392), I have dealt comprehensively with the editorial procedure of the evangelists. The historical process becomes the clearer in that one may trace the development of editorial technique from Mark to Matthew and Luke. While with Mark the art of the evangelist appears to be quite undeveloped, Luke displays a fine editorial artistry. Even the casual reader may note the difference if he will observe the quite distinct manners in which Matthew and Luke introduce material from the Sayings-document into Mark. Their problem was this: how to localize historically, and assign to a definite place in the life of Jesus, his sayings which had been collected without any reference to the place or time when they were spoken. Matthew solved the problem chiefly by introducing material from Q into appropriate scenes which he found in the Gospel of Mark. So, for example, he introduced the missionary directions addressed to the disciples in Chapter x into the scene of the sending out of the disciples which he found in Mark vi. Other directions addressed to the disciples (in Chapter xviii) he has introduced into the situation provided by the sayings on discipleship found in Mark ix. 33f. The polemic against the scribes and Pharisees in Chapter xxiii has been combined with Mark xii. 38–40. A whole series of eschatological sections in Chapters xxiv and xxv has been combined with Mark xiii — that is, he has added them on to Mark. Luke's method, on the contrary, has been as a rule to create new scenes out of typical material; for instance, the polemic against the Pharisees which he derived from the Sayings-document is developed into a separate dinner scene in xi. 37; the same sort of situation serves him also in Chapter xiv to localize a collection of sayings. The situation provided by Jesus' wandering journey toward Jerusalem furnishes him with the opportunity to bring forward the sayings on following Jesus (xiv. 25) and the parable of the entrusted pounds (xix. 11). Once trained to observation by the study of Matthew and Luke, whose methods are easier to recognize since comparison with Mark provides a constant criterion, one may discover a similar situation even in the Gospel of Mark. One may easily recognize, for example, that the motive of Jesus' withdrawing into the boat from the presence of the crowd is transferred by Mark from iv. 1, where it belonged with the traditional material, to iii. 9 where it stands in a totally unorganic relation; and that the motive of Jesus with the children has been carried back from x. 16, where it belongs to the older tradition, to ix. 36

where it remains a superfluous touch, serving only as an editorial introduction to the verse following. Similarly the analysis of Chapter iv shows that verses 10–13 form an editorial insertion of the evangelist, since here Jesus has retired with his disciples; while, on the other hand, verses 33ff. show that the situation presupposed at the beginning (vv. 1–2) still continues. The result is primarily negative, and we conclude that the whole framework of the history of Jesus must be viewed as an editorial construction, and that therewith a whole series of typical scenes, which because of their ecclesiastical use and their poetic and artistic associations we had looked upon as scenes in the life of Jesus, must be viewed as creations of the evangelists. On the other hand, it is certainly a positive gain that we may now recognize which parts of the gospels are derived from older traditional material.

But the task is not yet complete. For, in the first place, there is the possibility that these traditional sections may also have been edited by the evangelists; and in the second place, though they lay before the gospel writers as traditional material, it is not yet proved that they are historical narratives. It is at this point that we hope by means of the form-historical approach to make some further progress. This begins with the observation that, especially in primitive literature, literary expression (oral or written) makes use of more or less fixed forms, which have their own laws of style. In the Old Testament we have long been accustomed to recognize this feature and to apply the form-historical method. The forms of psalm, prayer, prophetic address, fable, story, and historical narrative have been recognized and their stylistic laws have been described. Is it possible to identify similar literary forms in the Synoptic tradition? If this be the case, one must recognize and reckon with the fact that the tradition possesses a certain solidity, since the form would naturally oppose itself to any serious alterations. On the other hand, it will be possible to determine in the individual sections whether the appropriate form was purely expressed or somewhat revised, and so one should be able to determine the age of the section. This would be the more true if it were possible to recognize not only the appropriate laws of style of a specified literary form but also the laws by which the further development of material takes place, *i.e.* a certain orderliness in change by which a body of tradition is always controlled in its growth. There are various means available to this end. The first is this, that we may accurately observe how the Marcan material is altered and revised by Matthew and Luke, and how Matthew and Luke have presumably edited the text of Q (the Sayings-document). If we are able to deduce a certain regularity in this procedure, then we may certainly assume that the same laws held good even earlier, and we may draw conclusions as to the state of the tradition prior to Mark and Q. It is clear that this is a very difficult process and one to be pursued with great caution. One may, however, test his skill by studying the manner in which the evangelic material was handed down in the later church, especially in the apocryphal gospels, and likewise the general laws governing popular narrative and tradition, such as stories and anecdotes. In order, however, to identify the peculiar stylistic laws governing the forms of the Synoptic tradition, we must remind ourselves that certain forms were found close at hand in the environment of the early Christian community, and offered themselves for purposes of tradition. Similar sayings and brief narratives were handed down in Jewish literature, and their forms show remarkable similarity to those of the evangelical material. Accordingly, the study of Jewish literature helps us to recognize the characteristic forms of the evangelic literature and the laws of style which govern them. A beginning has been made in this field of study within recent years. First there appeared the book by M. Dibelius, *The Form-History of the Gospel (Formgeschichte des Evangeliums,* 1919; second edition, 1933); then came my *History of the Synoptic Tradition (Geschichte der synoptischen Tradition,* 1921, second edition, 1931). Since then there have appeared, for example, a study of the Synoptic controversies by M. Albertz (*Die Synoptischen Streitgespräche,* 1921); one by G. Bertram on the Passion Narrative and the Christ cult (*Die Leidensgeschichte Jesu und der Christuskult,* 1922); an examination of the narrative style of the gospels by P. Fiebig (*Über den Erzählungsstil der Evangelien,* 1925); a study of the miracles by A. Fridrichsen (*Le Problème du Miracle,* 1925); and another by L. Brun on the Resurrection of Christ and the primitive Christian tradition (*Auferstehung Christi in der urchristlichen Überlieferung,* 1925). The general subject of the literary character of the gospels was handled in an essay by K. L. Schmidt (*Die Stellung der Evangelien in der allgemeinen Literaturgeschichte,* 1923, in the second volume of the *Festschrift* presented to H. Gunkel, under the title *Eucharisterion*). A critical treatment of Form-History is to be found in the book by E. Fascher, *The Form-historical Method* (*Die formgeschichtliche Methode,* 1924), and in L. Köhler's little work, *The Form-historical Problem of the New Testament* (*Das formgeschichtliche Problem des Neuen Testaments,* 1927). A good account of work in the field, and one useful for orientation, is that given by M. Dibelius in the *Theologische Rundschau,* new series, vol. i (1929), pp. 185–216. More recently there have appeared studies of the Nativity Narrative by M. Dibelius (*Jungfrauensohn und Krippenkind:* Sitzungsberichte der Heidelberger Akademie der Wissenschaften, Phil.-hist. Klasse, 1931–32, 4te Abhandlung), and by G. Erdmann (*Die Vorgeschichten des Lukas — und Matthäus-Evangeliums und Vergils vierte Ekloge,* 1932).

CHAPTER IV

THE LAWS GOVERNING POPULAR NARRATIVE AND TRADITION

The laws governing the formulation of popular narrative and tradition may be studied in detail in the material which the Synoptists hand down. The first thing we observe is that the narrators do not give us long unified accounts but rather small single pictures, individual scenes narrated with the utmost simplicity. These always occupy but a brief space of time; apart from the Passion Narrative no event or proceeding is narrated which covered more than two days. As a rule only two speaking characters appear in these scenes, or at most three; involved proceedings are beyond the powers of the simple story teller. Where groups or crowds are present, they are treated as a unity. As such narratives pass from mouth to mouth, or when one writer takes them over from another, their fundamental character remains the same, but the details are subject to the control of fancy and are usually made more explicit and definite. So, for example, Mark ix. 17 relates that the father brought his demoniac son to Jesus; in Luke's version is added the statement that he was an only son (ix. 38). The palsied hand which Jesus healed (Mark iii. 1) is described by Luke as the right hand (vi. 6). The ear of the high priest's servant which was struck off in Gethsemane (Mark xiv. 47) was accord-

ing to Luke xxii. 50 the right ear.   One may observe in
the account of this scene which appears in the Gospel
of John another important law at work: though the
Synoptists do not name either the servant or the
disciple who struck him, John gives the names, Malchus
and Peter.

In the apocryphal tradition the process may be followed still further since here legend creates the names
of hitherto unnamed persons; for example, those of the
three Wise Men from the East, the woman with an
issue of blood, the crucified robbers, the officer on guard
at Jesus' tomb, and so on.   However, one may see such
supplying of names already at work in the Synoptics.
The disciples who are sent to prepare for the Last Supper are unnamed in Mark (xiv. 13); in Luke their
names are given, Peter and John (xxii. 8).   Instead of
the disciples as in Mark vii. 17, it is Peter who asks the
question of Jesus in Matthew xv. 15.   The name of the
ruler of the synagogue, whose daughter Jesus raised
from death, is given as Jairus in Luke viii. 41; in Mark
there is a whole series of manuscripts in which the
name is omitted, and it is not at all unlikely that in the
others it was added to complete the text.   For this
reason one must be a little sceptical even of the names
given in Mark (e.g. x. 28, 46; xi. 21).

Still another example of the way in which fancy has
elaborated the older material is the account of the robbers crucified with Jesus (Luke xxiii. 39–43): Mark
knows nothing of this but says simply that the two men
crucified with Jesus mocked him (xv. 32).

Another characteristic trait is that the narrator pre-
fers to give in direct discourse what his source gave indirectly. For example, Mark viii. 32 states that when
Jesus announced his coming Passion, Peter upbraided
him; Matthew xvi. 22 reports him as saying, 'Be it far
from Thee, Lord!' Instead of the narrative of Mark
xiv. 1, 'After two days was the feast of the Passover and
of unleavened bread,' Matthew xxvi. 1 f reads, 'And it
came to pass when Jesus had finished all these sayings,
he said unto his disciples "Ye know that after two days
is the feast of the passover. . . ."' While Mark xiv. 23
relates that when the cup was passed around at the Last
Supper 'they all drank of it,' Matthew makes Jesus
say, 'Drink ye all of it' (xxvi. 27). In the account of
the kiss of Judas, Mark says nothing of any words of
Jesus; Matthew (xxvi. 50), however, and Luke (xxii.
48), each introduce a saying, though each brings forward
a different one — it is easy to see how imagination has
elaborated this scene. The last inarticulate cry of Jesus
(Mark xv. 37) becomes in Luke the saying, 'Father,
into Thy Hands I commend my spirit' (xxiii. 46).

Still another important fact deserves to be mentioned.
Along with the tendency to characterize more definitely
the dim figures in the tradition goes the inclination to
impose a schematic idea of the course of Jesus' activity,
viz. the opponents with whom Jesus engages in dis-
putation are almost invariably scribes and Pharisees,
who interrogate him with malicious intent. One may
often observe or infer that the earliest tradition had to
do with unspecified questioners, whom the later nar-

rators transformed into ill-disposed scribes or Pharisees. In the original Sayings-document (Q) it was only
stated that 'some of them' accused Jesus of collusion
with the devil (Luke xi. 15); according to Matthew
(xii. 24) these were Pharisees, according to Mark (iii.
22) they were scribes. Similarly the demand for a sign
was made originally by some of the crowd (Luke xi.
16); in Matthew (xii. 38) and Mark (viii. 11) the demand comes from the Pharisees (and scribes). It is
quite characteristic that Mark has retained in its old
form the story of the question concerning the greatest
commandment, in accordance with which the inquirer
is entirely honest, and in the end is praised by Jesus as
not far from the Kingdom of God (xii. 28-34). In
Matthew this word of praise has fallen away, and the
questioner appears from the outset as crafty and hypo-
critical (xxii. 34-40; cf. Luke x. 25). Of course, many
a polemical word of Jesus addressed to the scribes and
Pharisees may be entirely historical (Mark xii. 38-40;
and most of Matt. xxiii. 1-31), but the schematic representation according to which the Pharisees and scribes
are from the outset the sworn enemies of Jesus is certainly unhistorical.

CHAPTER V

THE VARIOUS TYPES OF TRADITIONAL MATERIAL

I. Miracle Stories

It may further be demonstrated that the evangelic material is set forth in the forms of distinct literary types. It is self-evident that the laws of style governing a literary type are more or less elastic; at the same time each type has its own definite characteristics which may be observed in every example of the type, even though these characteristics are not all present in any one example.

This may be seen for example in the miracle stories. Professor O. Weinreich has gathered together a body of material suitable for comparison under the title *Ancient Miracles of Healing* (*Antike Heilungswunder*, 1909), as have also P. Fiebig, *Jewish Miracle Narratives of the New Testament Period* (*Jüdische Wundergeschichten des neutestamentlichen Zeitalters*, 1911) and others. The lay reader may obtain an impression of such ancient miracle stories from a translation of the writing of Lucian of Samosata (second century A.D.), *The Friend of Lies* (Greek '*Philopseudes*').[1] A comparison of the two makes it clear that the miracle stories of the gospels possess a remarkable resemblance to the

Hellenistic miracle narratives; the latter accordingly throw significant light upon the problem of their origin or at least of their formulation.

The following seem to be characteristic of the style observed in the narratives of miracles. As a rule the narrative is given in three parts. First, the condition of the patient is described. Just as, for example, in Mark ix. 18 we read, ' I have brought unto thee my son who hath a dumb spirit; and wheresoever he taketh him, he teareth him: and he foameth and gnasheth with his teeth and pineth away ' — so Lucian tells the story (*Philops.* 16) of a certain 'Syrian from Palestine,' a ' wise man ' who had understanding in these matters: he was known to have healed many, ' who fell down in fits, rolled their eyes, and foamed at the mouth.' Typical also is the emphasis upon the gravity of the illness (e.g. Mark v. 3–5) or its long duration (e.g. Mark v. 25f; ix. 12; Luke xiii. 11). Just as in the Greek stories, so Mark v. 26 describes the futile efforts of physicians to heal the illness, and also the scornful attitude of the people when the true healer first appeared (Mark v. 40). Just as here it is said that the crowd standing about the house of mourning laughed Jesus to scorn, so, for example, the inscriptions in the temple of the healing God Asclepios at Epidauros tell of a sick woman who laughed sceptically when she heard of the marvellous deeds of the God, or how the crowd ridiculed the folly of a man totally blind who hoped for divine healing.

In the second section of the story the healing itself

is narrated. Often the peculiar manipulations of the healer are described, as in Mark vii. 33; viii. 23. In general, however, the New Testament miracle stories are extremely reserved in this respect, since they hesitate to attribute to the person of Jesus the magical traits which were often characteristic of the Hellenistic miracle worker. In Hellenistic stories we are told, for example, how an exorcist drove the spirit out of a demoniac by holding a ring to the patient's nose so that he might smell a marvellous root that has been set in it; or how another healed a person of snake-bite by placing upon the wounded foot a tiny piece of the gravestone of a virgin, to the accompaniment of an appropriate magic formula. In the gospels as a rule it is simply stated, as likewise in the Hellenistic narratives, that the wonder worker approaches the patient — perhaps coming to his bedside — lays his hand upon him or takes him by the hand and utters the healing word. It is also characteristic that these words are as a rule given in an unknown foreign tongue, like 'Talitha kumi' (Mark v. 41) and 'Ephphatha' (Mark vii. 34). Where the view prevails that the patient is possessed by a demon we are told how the demon sensed the presence of his master, disputed with him, but was finally threatened and driven out, as in the genuine folk-tale contained in Mark v. 1–20. Finally, it may be noted as characteristic that not infrequently it is said that no one was present at the miracle proper; e.g. Mark vii. 33; viii. 23. We find some examples in the Old Testament: I Kings xvii. 19; II Kings iv. 4, 33. The original implication of this is doubtless that no one may witness an act of deity, as in the story of Lot's wife (Genesis xix. 26).

Two characteristics are found in the third section, as a rule. First of all it was naturally often pointed out that witnesses of the wonderful results of the miracles broke out in exclamations of wonder or approval. Not infrequently it is related of the person healed that he gave some clear demonstration of the fact: for example, the lame man taking up his bed and walking, as in Mark ii. 11f, and in a miracle story that Lucian relates. To the same effect is the statement that the restored daughter of Jairus was given something to eat (Mark v. 43); by this anyone could see that she was completely restored to life. Following the exorcism of demons the demonstration often consists in some spiteful and destructive act of the departing demon, like the shattering of a pillar or the overturning of a bowl of water, or, as in Mark v. 13, the sudden frenzy of a herd of swine who dash over a cliff and fall into the sea.

II. Apothegms

Among the sayings of Jesus it is possible to distinguish various groups. There are those, for example, which have been handed down in association with a little scene, in which according to the tradition they were originally spoken. Dibelius calls such fragments of tradition 'paradigms,' since he assumes that they served as illustrations in Christian preaching. I prefer to call them apothegms, since in their structure they are closely related to the narratives of Greek literature which have

hitherto borne this name. It is characteristic that the
narrated scene serves only as the framework for an important saying; the whole point lies in the saying, and
the frame simply gives the situation in which the word
was spoken, and its occasion. The occasion may be the
question of a disciple or a scribe; and the question, in
turn, may have been occasioned by some deed of Jesus
such as a healing on the Sabbath, or by the conduct of
the disciples who ate without first performing the ritual
washing of hands. In such a classification belong the
controversies of the Synoptic tradition, such as those in
Mark ii. 1–12, 23–28; iii. 1–6; vii. 1–23 etc.; conversations
with eager inquirers, as in Mark x. 17–22; xii. 28:34;
Matthew xi. 2–19; Luke xvii. 20–21 etc.; and scenes of a
biographical character, like Mark vi. 1–6; x. 13–16; Luke
ix. 57–62; xi. 27–28 etc. Such apothegms are to be found
in Jewish literature as well as in Greek, but a closer
consideration shows that there were characteristic differences between Jewish and Greek literature on this
point. For the Jewish story, it is significant that the
saying of the hero which is given in response to a
question usually appears either as a counter-question
or as a brief parable (or both at once). This is true of
most of the apothegms of Jesus. A story of Rabban
Gamaliel may serve as a Jewish example (Fiebig,
Erzählungsstil, p. 103). A heathen philosopher once
asked him why it was that God should be angered at
idolatry, and he replied: ' Suppose a man calls his dog
by the name of his father, and when he makes a vow
uses the words, " By the life of this dog"; with whom

will the father be angry, with the son or with the dog?'
Another example is a dispute over the resurrection of
the dead (Strack-Billerbeck, *Kommentar* I, p. 895):
'The Emperor Hadrian said to Rabban Gamaliel, "You
say that the dead will come back to life again; on the
contrary they have turned to dust, and can dust come
to life again?" Then Gamaliel's daughter spoke up
and said to her father, "Never mind, let me answer
him! In our city," she said, "there were two potters.
One made his vessels out of water and the other out of
clay. Which of these two deserves the greater praise?"
The Emperor replied, "The one who made vessels out
of water," and she said, "If God is able to create a man
out of moisture, how much more can he do so out of
clay!"' This is the way the Synoptic controversies go.
For example, Jesus replies (Mark ii. 19) to the question,
why his disciples do not fast, with the parabolic question, 'Do the sons of the bride-chamber (the bridegroom's companions) fast while the bridegroom is still
with them?' To the invidious question whether or
not he will heal on the Sabbath (Mark iii. 4), he replies
with the counter-question, 'Is it lawful to do good on
the Sabbath day, or to do evil?' Similar counter-
questions and parables are given in reply to the accusa-
tion of collusion with Satan in Mark iii. 24–26 (cf. Mark
ii. 25f; xi. 30; Luke xiii. 15, xiv. 5; Matthew xvii. 25).
One may safely infer that these narratives have almost
all been formulated in a Jewish environment and do
not belong to the later Hellenistic period of development.

It is characteristic of the Greek apothegm that it is
introduced with some such formula as, 'When he was
asked by . . . ,' or 'Once when he observed how. . . .'
We may give an example or two of this style. 'When
asked by the Tyrant Dionysius why it was that philosophers visited the rich rather than the rich the philosophers, Aristippus replied: "The philosophers realize
what they lack, but the rich do not."' 'Anaxagoras of
Klazomenai, when he was asked why we are here, replied, "To behold the works of nature."' 'Once when
Demonax saw two philosophers engaged in a thoroughly discreditable argument, in which one of them
asked foolish questions, and the other replied with ir-
relevancies, he said, "My friends, do you not realize
that one of you is milking a ram and the other is holding up a sieve?"' 'As Diogenes once saw a child
drinking out of its hands, he threw away the cup that
he had in his wallet and said, "A child has exceeded
me in doing without things."'[2]   The passage in Luke
xvii. 20–21 is formulated in this manner: 'And when he
was demanded of the Pharisees, when the Kingdom of
God should come, he answered them and said, "The
Kingdom of God cometh not with observation: neither
shall they say, Lo here! or lo there! for, behold, the
Kingdom of God is [at once] among you."' Similar
to this is the narrative contained in one manuscript of
Luke vi. 5: 'On the same day when he saw a man
working on the Sabbath he said to him, "Man, if you
know what you are doing, you are happy! but if you do
not know, then you are accursed and a breaker of the

law."' It may accordingly be concluded that these
two accounts were first formulated in the Hellenistic
church. However, it is not only possible but really
probable that in Luke xvii. 20–21 only the framework,
the scene, is a later creation and that the saying of Jesus
is derived from the older tradition. One must therefore distinguish carefully between those apothegms in
which the framework and the saying are so closely related that one cannot be told without the other (e.g.
Mark ii. 18–19; iii. 1–5; Luke xii. 13–14 — ' And one of
the company said unto him, " Master speak to my
brother, that he divide the inheritance with me," but
he said unto him, " Man, who made me a judge or a
divider over you? " '), and others, in which the framework and the saying are only loosely connected.
Among the latter it is often only the saying of Jesus
which is original and the frame has been supplied later;
e.g. Mark vii. 1–23; x. 2–12. Especially significant is
Mark ii. 15–17. Jesus' saying reads, ' They that are
whole have no need of the physician but they that are
sick; I came not to call the righteous but sinners;' the
setting in vv. 15f. has been artistically supplied later.
This is indicated by the wholly unmotivated, and literally impossible, appearance of the Pharisaic scribes at
a dinner attended by publicans, and further by the remarkable fact that it is the disciples who are questioned
and Jesus who replies — and the same is true of other
sayings in the series. The effort was made to introduce
the traditional words of Jesus as completely as possible
into scenes in his life, and in this case the setting of a

meal seemed to be the most appropriate situation, since
fellowship at table easily symbolized fellowship in general. One may further observe in other cases that un-
attached sayings of Jesus have been introduced into
older apothegms or fastened on to them; examples of
the former are found in Matt. xii. 11f; Luke xiv. 5; of
the latter in Mark ii. 27f; vii. 9–23; x. 23–27.

Striking also is a further observation that may be
made: in Mark ii. 18–19, 23–26; vii. 1–8, it is related that
the disciples did not fast, that they rubbed out kernels
of grain on the Sabbath, and that they did not observe
the ritual washing before meals. How are we to explain the fact that all these things are told of the disciples and not of Jesus himself, and that Jesus is called
upon to defend their conduct rather than his own? It
is impossible to assume that in all these instances his
own conduct was correct; for the disciples can have
learned their free attitude only from him! Nor may
one suppose that the opponents hesitated to attack him
directly; since in other cases, e.g. with reference to the
healings on the Sabbath, they had no such hesitation.

Apparently the situation is to be understood only as
follows: these traditions first arose in the Christian community and are to be explained by its situation. The
'disciples,' i.e. the primitive Christian church, have
broken with the old customs in this matter, and they
are defending themselves against criticism by means
of the stories, through which they make their appeal
to a saying of Jesus. It is certainly possible that the

saying of Jesus enshrined in such a setting is old and authentic, as, for example, probably Mark ii. 19. In the other cases it is less probable, since here argumentative use is made of sentences from the Old Testament, and since most of the words of Jesus which cite the Old Testament are suspected of originating in the theological debates of the primitive community. Just as in this primitive community the faith in Jesus as the Messiah was defended by an appeal to Old Testament passages, so likewise an effort was made to found Christian practice upon a similar appeal.

Those apothegms which are of a biographical character are likewise for the most part creations of the community, since they give expression to what Christians had experienced of their Master or what he had experienced at the hands of his people. It is accordingly clear that the calling of the disciples in Mark i. 16–20 reflects no historical situation; the story completely lacks motivation and psychological probability. The scene sets forth symbolically and picturesquely the common experience of the disciples as they were raised by Jesus' wonderful power out of their previous spheres of life. It is in this way that we must also explain Mark iii. 31–35 (Jesus' true relatives); xii. 41–44 (the widow's mite); Luke ix. 57–62 (various followers); x. 38–42 (Mary and Martha). Even the scene in Nazareth (Mark vi. 1–6) may perhaps not reflect a particular historical event, but is rather a symbolical picture, setting forth the attitude of the people as a whole to the

preaching of Jesus. As evidence for this may be cited
the saying of Jesus found in one of the papyri:

'No prophet is welcome in his own home town;
And no physician can cure those who know him well.'

It may be that the scene in Mark has been created out
of this saying.

III. WORDS OF JESUS: THEIR FATE IN THE COURSE OF TRADITION

Even though we must give up the historicity of many
of these narratives, still it remains possible, and even
probable, that in many cases the saying of Jesus which
they contain is thoroughly historical. Thus we arrive
at the question whether or not there are evidences which
will enable us to distinguish, within the words of Jesus
so handed down, between what is old and authentic and
what has been produced later. It is, of course, of fundamental importance to observe that many of these traditional words derive their meaning from their context.
The words, ' Agree with thine adversary quickly whiles
thou art in the way with him, etc.,' appear in Matthew
v. 25–26 as an admonition to reconciliation; in Luke xii.
57–59 they become a parable of warning: Just as a man
in his earthly life will endeavor to avoid a process at
law, even at the last moment, through reconciliation
with his opponent, since no one can tell how things
will turn out at court, so everyone should take care
while there is still time not to appear as a defendant
before the throne of the heavenly Judge. It is probable

that the latter form retains the original sense of the words. In other cases we no longer know what was originally meant, since the original occasion and the historical connection of the words are unknown, and the context in which the evangelist has placed them rests upon a very uncertain interpretation. What, for example, was the original meaning of the words concerning Salt and concerning Light? In Matthew v. 13-15 both sayings appear as a parable on the calling of the disciples. In Mark the saying concerning Salt appears without any interpretation (ix. 50), that concerning Light is definitely interpreted as a saying about evangelism (iv. 21). We are not certain just what meaning Luke attached to the saying about Light (xi. 33); the Salt, which has lost its power to season, he interprets of disciples who lack the courage to sacrifice all they possess in following Jesus (xiv. 34-35). These examples show that the interpretations of the evangelists are experiments, now and then no doubt quite correct, but at any rate providing no guarantee of the original meaning.

One may see this most clearly of all in the parables. What the parables of the Tower-builder and the King declaring war were originally meant to teach (Luke xiv. 28-32), we have no means of knowing, since the interpretation which Luke gives (xiv. 33) rests solely upon his own conjecture. Unrecognizable also is the original sense of the words about the new patch on the old garment and about the new wine in the old skins, which Mark has attached to the discussion on

fasting (ii. 21-22); likewise the original sense of the
parables of the Mustard-seed and the Leaven (Matthew
xiii. 31-33) and still others. It is precisely in the tradition of the parables that the fate of the Lord's sayings
can be most clearly observed. Jülicher has shown in
his great work on *The Parables of Jesus*[3] that the Christian community and the evangelists have often misin-
terpreted the parables, for the reason that they looked
upon them as allegories secretly setting forth in advance
the destiny of Jesus or that of his followers; while the
truth is that the parables were not designed originally
to conceal anything but to make something clear — by
means of a story based upon everyday human affairs or
relations, requiring an exercise of judgment on the part
of the hearer, and urging him to apply this same judgment in the realm of the spiritual life, with which it is
really concerned.

While in an allegory the largest possible number of
details are given a secret meaning, in a parable there
is only one striking point (the *tertium comparationis*)
to look for. For this reason the verses in Mark iv. 10-12,
in which the purpose of the parables is described as con-
cealment, must be ascribed to the dogmatic theory of
the evangelist. Similarly the interpretations of the
parable of the Sower, given in Mark iv. 14-20, and of
the Tares among the wheat, given in Matthew xiii.
36-43, must be viewed as later additions. Accordingly,
the parable of the Ten Virgins in Matthew xxv. 1-13
is similarly to be viewed as a later allegory, though perhaps founded upon an older parable. As a rule, it is

fairly easy to remove the allegorical traces from a parable. To the parabolic saying in Mark ii. 19, 'Can the children of the bride-chamber fast, while the bridegroom is with them?' is added in verse 20 the allegorical prediction of the death of Jesus and the later Christian practice of fasting. In the parable of the Banquet in Matthew xxii. 1–10 = Luke xiv. 16–24, Matthew has introduced, in v. 7, a prediction of the destruction of Jerusalem. Luke, on the contrary, since he has added on at the end a second invitation addressed to new guests, has made this an allegorical prediction of the Gentile Mission; finally Matthew (vv. 11–14) has added an allegorical supplement relating to the moral worthiness of members of the Christian community. With the parable of the Entrusted Talents (Matthew xxv. 14–30 = Luke xix. 12–27), Luke has combined an allegory of the departing and returning King who mercilessly punishes the rebels who have risen against him in his absence — a prediction of the coming Judgment.

In the interpretation of the parables, the student is greatly assisted not only by a comparison of the Synoptic parallels but also by a study of the style observed in rabbinic parables; these have a close relation to those of Jesus, and clearly demonstrate that the interpretation of the parables as predictive allegories is a false one.[4]

Still other sayings of our Lord have been considerably transformed and enlarged by the evangelists, whether in the interests of continuity, or for the purpose of introducing some reference to the person of Jesus or a prophecy relating to the community. In Luke xii. 3 the same saying is handed down as in Matthew x. 27. In the Lucan formulation it reads, 'Therefore whatsoever ye have spoken in darkness shall be heard in the light and that which ye have spoken in the ear in closets shall be proclaimed upon the house-tops.' The saying, like the one which precedes it (Luke xii. 2 = Matt. x. 26; the same saying is found in Mark iv. 22), is a proverb with the same sense as the German one,

> 'Nothing is so finely spun
> It quite escapes the light of the sun.'

In the connection which Luke gives it this is a word of reassurance addressed to the apostles: their preaching, however modest its beginnings, will nevertheless win the whole world. In Matthew the saying reads, 'What I tell you in darkness, that speak ye in light: and what ye hear in the ear that preach ye upon the housetops.' Clearly, Matthew has altered the saying, and out of the proverb has created Jesus' commission of his disciples to preach. Another example is the saying about confession of faith in Jesus. The history of this saying may be traced, inasmuch as it is given both in Mark (viii. 38) and in the Sayings-document (Q: Luke xii. 8–9 = Matt. x. 32–33). Since the text of Luke is closer to that of Mark than is Matthew's, one must conclude that Luke has retained the older form of the saying more accurately than Matthew has done, and that the latter has altered it. Originally this saying ran, 'Whosoever confesses Jesus (and his words), him also will the Son of Man sometime confess;' Jesus clearly distinguishing himself from the Son of Man (as he does also in Matt. xxiv. 27, 37 = Luke xvii. 24, 26, and elsewhere, speaking of the Son of Man in the third person); but since for the Christian community it was axiomatic that Jesus himself was the Son of Man, the old form of the words was not retained, and it may be readily understood how Matthew came to make Jesus say: 'Whosoever therefore shall confess me before men, him will *I* confess.'

Just as this saying was worked over under the influence of the faith of the community, so also, for example, was the saying about seeking signs (Luke xi. 29–30 = Matt. xii. 38–40). According to the form which Luke gives the saying Jesus accredited himself, as did once the prophet Jonah, by means of the sign of the preaching of repentance; according to Matthew the sign consists in Jonah's three days in the belly of the fish, i.e. the death of Jesus and his resurrection after three days which were thus predicted.

In other places changes have been occasioned by considerations of literary form. Of the six great antitheses in Matthew v. 21–48 ('Ye have heard that it was said . . . but I say unto you'), only three possessed this antithetic form originally, viz. those concerning murder, adultery, and oaths. Following this model the three other sayings, concerning divorce, revenge, and love of enemies, have been created out of older sayings of our Lord whose original form may now be recognized from Luke xvi. 18 (cf. Mark x. 11–12) and Luke vi. 27–35. The contrast may easily be recognized: the sayings regarding murder, adultery, and oaths all take an Old Testament prohibition as a theme; but they cannot repudiate it, they simply outbid it. The sayings concerning divorce, revenge, and love of enemies attach themselves to an Old Testament law which is not a prohibition but a concession, and they frankly repudiate it. As these words appear in Luke, they altogether lack this antithetic formulation. Still another example is Luke xxi. 20–24, where the evangelist has so completely altered the Marcan original (xiii. 14–20) that the text becomes a prediction of the siege and destruction of Jerusalem in the year 70 A.D.

Not only have many of the older sayings of Jesus been modified in the course of tradition, but not seldom words have been placed in Jesus' mouth which in reality were either spoken by other Jewish teachers or first arose in the Christian community. How such words got into the tradition will be explained when we consider now the three classes of Jesus' words which are distinguished in form-historical research.

IV. Words of Jesus: Proverbs

One group of the transmitted sayings are ' proverbs ' in the narrower sense, i.e. words of wisdom, aphorisms such as circulated in Israel and in Judaism and throughout the Orient generally, not only among the people but chiefly among the teachers of wisdom — in Judaism the rabbis. Examples of this type of literature are found in the so-called *Proverbs of Solomon* in the Old Testament, and in the *Wisdom of Jesus the Son of Sirach* in the Apocrypha. Among the words of Jesus belonging in this classification are: 'Out of the abundance of the heart the mouth speaketh' (Matt. xii. 34b); 'Sufficient unto the day is the evil thereof' (Matt. vi. 34b); 'For wheresoever the carcase is, there will the eagles be gathered together' (Matt. xxiv. 28); and likewise the words and sayings found in Luke xii. 2, 3 (cf. Mark iv. 22) discussed above, and others, such as the sayings regarding the laying up of treasures, the service of Mammon, and anxiety, in Matthew vi. 19–34. The majority of these sayings have parallels in the Jewish Wisdom literature. Thus the little story of the rich farmer in Luke xii. 16–20 is closely related to Sirach xi. 18, 19:

'There is that waxeth rich by his wariness and
      pinching,
And this is the portion of his reward:
When he saith, I have found rest,
And now will I eat of my goods;
Yet he knoweth not what time shall pass,
And he shall leave them to others, and die.'

One may compare the form though not the contents of Matthew vi. 19–30 with the passage in Proverbs vi. 6–8; and, for contents, the rabbinic saying, 'Hast thou ever seen beast or bird working at a trade? Nevertheless they support themselves without cares.' One may compare Luke xiv. 7–11 with Proverbs xxv. 6–7.

Luke xiv. 7–11:

'. . . When thou art bidden of any man to a wedding, sit not down in the highest room; lest a more honourable man than thou be bidden of him; and he that bade thee and him come and say to thee, " Give this man place; " and thou begin with shame to take the lowest room. But when thou art bidden, go and sit down in the lowest room; that when he that bade thee cometh, he may say unto thee, " Friend, go up higher: " then shalt thou have worship in the presence of them that sit at meat with thee. For whosoever exalteth himself shall be abased; and he that humbleth himself shall be exalted.'

Proverbs xxv. 6–7:

' Put not thyself forward in the presence of the king,
And stand not in the place of great men:
For better is it that it be said unto thee,
     " Come up hither,"
Than that thou shouldest be put lower in the presence of the prince.'

Mark viii. 37 had originally the meaning that life itself is the highest good, as in the Oriental proverb, ' You may easily trade land with another; but there is no exchange for a life.' With Matthew vi. 24 one may compare the Oriental saying, ' No one can carry two melons in one hand.' With Mark iv. 21 one may compare another: ' You don't beat a drum under a rug.'

Again, the sentence 'Every hour has troubles enough of its own,' which affords a parallel to Matthew vi. 34b, is found more than once in the rabbinic literature. Indeed, this class of proverbial sayings has so many analogies in the rabbinic literature that one may even say, ' Not one of the ethical precepts of Jesus was, or needed to be, entirely unique.' [5]

Now it is naturally possible that Jesus himself originated some of the Wisdom-sayings which the gospels record as spoken by him. It is equally possible that he made use now and then of proverbs which were current in his time. But it is quite clear that we must reckon with the possibility that the primitive community placed in his mouth many a beautiful saying that was really derived from the treasure of Jewish proverbial lore. This is even suggested by the fact that most of these sayings appear in contexts where the application gives them explicit significance (e.g. Luke xii. 2, 3; Mark iv. 21, 22; viii. 37; Matt. xii. 30; xxiv. 28). Moreover, since the context or connection was really created by the later tradition (chiefly by the evangelists themselves), one must consider the question whether such Wisdom-sayings were not first admitted to the collection of Jesus' sayings at the time when, under the stress of the community's own needs, connected discourses of Jesus were first produced. At any rate, it is these Wisdom-sayings that are least guaranteed to be authentic words of Jesus; and they are likewise the least characteristic and significant for historical interpretation.

V. Words of Jesus: Prophetic and
Apocalyptic Sayings

A second group of the words of Jesus is formed by
the prophetic and apocalyptic sayings, in which Jesus
proclaimed the arrival of the Reign of God and
preached the call to repentance, promising salvation
for those who were prepared and threatening woes
upon the unrepentant. Here belong Luke x. 23f =
Matthew xiii. 16f, the felicitation of his contemporaries who are eye-witnesses of the fulfilment of prophecy;
further Matthew xi. 5–6 = Luke vii. 22–23, the description of the coming of the era of salvation; and, more
important still, Luke vi. 20–21 = Matthew v. 3–9, the
Beatitudes of the Sermon on the Mount. In the same
classification belong Luke xii. 8–9 (cf. Mark viii. 38)
the saying about witnessing for Jesus, the sayings about
the scribes in Matthew xxiii and Luke xi, and the prediction of the destruction of the temple in Mark xiii. 2.
The sayings are distinguished by their brevity and vigor
and have their parallels in ancient prophecy, not in contemporary apocalyptic. They are obviously not typical
products of apocalyptic fancy, but original utterances
of a prophetic personality. One may with perfect right
recognize among them authentic words of Jesus; and
though the Christian community itself produced many
a prophetic saying, as may be clearly shown, it must
nevertheless be recognized that, according to the testi-
mony of the earliest Christians themselves, they owed

their eschatological enthusiasm to the prophetic appearance of Jesus.

It must, however, be recognized on the other hand
that in the Christian community after Jesus' death the
prophetic spirit was alive. We know from the later
tradition that prophets appeared in the community
and spoke in Jesus' name. Such words of Christian
prophets are those, for example, in Revelation iii. 20,
'Behold, I stand at the door, and knock . . . ;' Revelation xvi. 15, 'Behold, I come as a thief . . .' It now
seems probable that some of the prophetic sayings in
the gospels were really derived from Christian prophets
and were afterward attributed to the historical Jesus;
for example, Matthew x. 16a, 'Behold, I send you
forth as sheep in the midst of wolves;' Luke x. 19-20,
'Behold, I give unto you power to tread on serpents
and scorpions . . . ;' so also Matthew xvi. 18-19; xviii.
20, and the Great Commission in Matthew xxviii. 19-20;
Luke xxiv. 49. Authentic sayings of Jesus have been
supplemented in this manner; thus the benediction of
the persecuted in Luke vi. 22-23 = Matthew v. 10-12
is an elaboration of the old Beatitudes made at a time
when the community was persecuted. But even in
this group sayings are found which the church took
over from Jewish tradition and with certain alterations and additions attributed to Jesus. Thus the discourse in Mark xiii. 5-27 is obviously a little Jewish
apocalypse which has been Christianized by giving it
certain additions (vv. 5-6; 9-11; 13; 24); similarly

Luke xi. 49–51 (= Matt. xxiii. 34–36) and xiii. 34–5 (= Matt. xxiiii. 37–39) probably originated in some Jewish writing.

VI. Words of Jesus: Sayings Concerning the Law

Finally, a third group is formed by Jesus' words regarding the Law, to which have been attached many sayings setting forth the regulations of the community. To these sayings about the Law belong the words concerning purity (Mark vii. 15); concerning divorce (Mark x. 11–12); the antitheses in Matthew v. 21–22, 27–28, 33–37; the sayings concerning alms-giving, prayer, and fasting in Matthew vi. 2–18. Once more we are dealing with sayings which have their true parallel in the preaching of the old prophets against external piety. In their flaming opposition to legalistic piety they cannot have originated within contemporary Judaism, even though here and there an individual teacher expressed the spirit of a broader religion, nor out of the community, since here we observe a steady tendency in the direction of legalism. Though the formulation of one or another of them may be due to the church, as a whole these words of conflict with legalism, and expressing a spiritual obedience to the will of God, go back to the prophetic personality to whom the church owed its existence, that is to the personality of Jesus. Even though many of the sayings may have originated in the community, the spirit that lives in them goes back to the work of Jesus.

Somewhat less confidently one may judge the Old

Testament citations which are frequently found in combination with these controversial sayings, e.g. Matthew xii. 5–6; Mark vii. 9–13; x. 6–9; they may have originated in the community, which was now defending, with Scripture citations, its new spiritual possession against the attacks of its Jewish opponents. Especially significant are the sayings which contain rules for the discipline of the community and for its mission, which probably all originated in the early church. Examples of these are Matthew xvi. 18–19 (Peter's power of the keys); xviii. 15–22 (directions for church discipline, etc.; cf. with this passage the more original form in Luke xviii. 3–4); Matthew x. 5–16 (directions for the church's mission); and, further, the passages which first arose in the Gentile Christian community, as their style shows, e.g. Mark vii. 20–23 (the explanation of the saying regarding purity); Luke xxi. 34–36 (the exhortation to watchfulness). In addition to these may be mentioned the sayings in which the church expressed its faith in Jesus, his work, his destiny, and his person. The Passion-predictions of Mark viii. 31; ix. 31; x. 33–34 and elsewhere were first created by the Christian community; so likewise perhaps were all, or at least most, of the other words which spoke of Jesus' coming, such as Matthew v. 17, 'Think not that I am come to destroy the Law, or the prophets: I am not come to destroy but to fulfil.' Similarly, Mark x. 45, 'For even the Son of Man came not to be ministered unto, but to minister, and to give his life a ransom for many.' These sayings express a reflective and retrospective point of view,

from which the interpretation of the life of Jesus as a
whole has become possible.

VII. Words of Jesus: The Question of Authenticity

The investigation of the sayings of Jesus leads to a
considerable uncertainty, but it does not end finally
in complete scepticism. By no means are we at the
mercy of those who doubt or deny that Jesus ever lived.
One must clearly recognize, of course, that what we
are dealing with in the tradition is, first of all, the earliest community. We recognize further that this community displays characteristic traits of a new spirit,
and, exercising its own historically distinctive powers,
sets itself free from Judaism; last of all we observe that
this society is aware that it owes its existence and its
spiritual possessions to the work of Jesus. It is through
the medium of the community, accordingly, that the
figure of the historical Jesus appears. Though we cannot now define with certainty the extent of the authentic words of Jesus, we are nevertheless able to distinguish the various levels of tradition; and when, by
a process of careful historical investigation, we distinguish the secondary layers in the tradition, what
results is not, like the peeling of an onion, a reduction
to nothingness — since the farther one goes the nearer
one comes to the center, which holds the secret of its
historical power. The layers which lie about this center
may be viewed as its historical results, either as its direct consequence or as a partial effect due to its contact
with religious material of another kind. It cannot be

denied that even here many uncertainties remain, and
that the historical work still to be done at this point is
neither complete, nor can ever arrive at absolutely certain results; but if the work is done in accordance with
clear methods, it cannot result in complete scepticism.
On one point one must rest content: the *character* of
Jesus, the vivid picture of his personality and his life,
cannot now be clearly made out; but, what is more important, the content of his message is or will be ever
more clearly recognizable.   Though one may admit
the fact that for no single word of Jesus is it possible to
produce positive evidence of its authenticity, still one
may point to a whole series of words found in the oldest stratum of tradition which do give us a consistent
representation of the historical message of Jesus.   These
are the prophetic words, echoing the call to repentance:

' For whosoever will save his life, shall lose it;
    But whosoever shall lose his life [for my sake and
        the gospel's], the same shall save it ' (Mark viii.
        35).
' Let the dead bury their dead: but go thou and
        preach the kingdom of God ' (Luke ix. 60).
' No man, having put his hand to the plough, and
        looking back, is fit for the Kingdom of God '
        (Luke ix. 62).

The same may be said of the following: Luke xi.
31–32 ('Here is one greater than Solomon, than
Jonah'); xii. 54–56 (the signs of the time); xiv. 26–27
(sayings about discipleship and bearing the cross);

Matthew vii. 13–14 (the narrow gate); the sayings
which announce the coming salvation, such as the Beatitudes pronounced upon the poor, the hungry, and them
that weep in Luke vi. 20–21; or the saying in Luke x.
23–24 (= Matt. xiii. 16–17):

> ' Blessed are the eyes which see the things that ye
>   see!
> For I tell you,
> That many prophets and kings have desired to see
>   those things which ye see, and have not seen
>   them;
> And to hear those things which ye hear, and have
>   not heard them! '

Similar are the words regarding the joy at a marriage
(Mark ii. 19a), the binding of the ' strong man ' (Mark
iii. 27), and those about the coming of the Kingdom of
God as evidenced by the exorcism of demons (Matt.
xii. 28). Here also belongs Matthew xi. 5–6:

> ' The blind receive their sight, and the lame walk,
>   the lepers are cleansed and the deaf hear,
>   the dead are raised up, and the poor have the gospel
>   preached to them,
>   and blessed is he, whosoever shall not be offended
>   in me! '

Similarly the words which express the consciousness of
a prophet, that he has been sent in the last decisive hour
—such as the words, just cited, in Matthew xi. 5–6.
Further, we have in Mark viii. 38, the saying, ' Whoso-

ever therefore shall be ashamed of me and of my words in this adulterous and sinful generation, of him also shall the Son of Man be ashamed, when he cometh in the glory of his Father with the holy angels.' Or: 'Why call ye me, Lord, Lord, and do not the things which I say?' (Luke vi. 46). The sayings which counsel purity of heart, sincere obedience and child-likeness, such as Mark vii. 15, 'There is nothing from without a man, that entering into him can defile him: but the things which come out of him, those are they that defile the man;' Mark iii. 4, 'Is it lawful to do good on the Sabbath day, or to do evil? to save life, or to kill?' Matthew v. 39b–41 (foregoing revenge); 44–48 (love of enemies); xxiii. 16–19 (against taking oaths lightly); 23–24 (straining at a gnat and swallowing a camel); 25–26 (external and inward cleanness); Mark x. 15: 'Verily I say unto you, Whosoever shall not receive the Kingdom of God as a little child, he shall not enter therein!'

CHAPTER VI

THE GOSPELS AS A WHOLE: WORSHIP, EVANGELISM, LEGEND, THE THREE EVANGELISTS

It is out of the individual fragments of tradition, as they have been viewed in the preceding sections, that the narrative of the work of Jesus contained in the gospels has been woven together. They do not, however, give a complete account of its historical course such as would enable us to see the causes and effects, the inner connections and developments. It is perfectly clear that it was not the historical interest that dominated, but the needs of Christian faith and life. One may designate the final motive by which the gospels were produced as the *cultic* (that is, the needs of common worship), if one considers that the high point of Christian life was the gathering of the community for worship, when the figure of Jesus, his teaching as well as his life, was set forth before the eyes of the faithful, and when accordingly the gospels served for public reading. For Christian preaching in the Hellenistic world, it was the death and resurrection of Jesus, viewed as a unity, which was the decisive event in the progress of salvation. This is shown by the brief predictions of Jesus woven together in the Gospel of Mark, in which he sets forth to his disciples the secret of his own person (Mark viii. 31; ix. 31; x. 32-34), as also, and especially, the succinct formulations of the Christian message in certain of the addresses in the Book of Acts (ii. 22-23, here expanded by means of Scriptural proofs; iii. 13-15; x. 37-43; xiii. 26-31). They also show that the preacher as a rule led up to his words about Jesus' suffering, death and resurrection by a review of his work (ii. 22; x. 37-39). Out of such preaching grew the gospels, as gradually the single fragments of tradition, which told of Jesus' words and deeds, were drawn into this framework. Since the main emphasis lay upon the conclusion, the Passion and the Easter story, it has quite correctly been said, 'With some exaggeration one might describe the gospels as Passion Narratives with extended introductions' (M. Kähler).

In view of the importance of the Passion Narrative, it is quite conceivable that a continuous account of its events would be handed down at a very early period, in which Jesus' arrest in Gethsemane, his condemnation by the Jewish court and by Pilate, the way to the cross, his crucifixion and death, were briefly told. Such an account appears to underlie the Passion Narrative of Mark. But, as it appears in Mark, and probably even before him, the narrative has been given its form in the interests of the cultus, its individual episodes being composed for purposes of edification. This is even more apparent in Matthew and Luke, where the Marcan narrative is expanded and additional episodes are supplied; thus, for example, we have the picture of Jesus and the

weeping women of Jerusalem on the way to Golgotha
(Luke xxiii. 27–31), the death of Judas (Matt. xxvii.
3–10), and the setting of a watch at the grave (Matt.
xxvii. 62–66). It is not only pious fancy which is at
work here, but also the apologetic interest. This is
especially noticeable in the effort of the evangelists to
shift the blame from the Roman authorities to the Jews,
as e.g. in the account of Pilate washing his hands (Matt.
xxvii. 24–25). The main point, however, is that the
whole narrative has been composed from the point of
view of faith and worship: it was as the Messiah, the
Son of God, that Jesus suffered and died. In Gethsemane he offered up his will to God and became obedi-
ent even unto the death of the cross; while marvellous
signs clearly show, at the end, that his death was a
world-transforming catastrophe.[1]

It is equally clear that the Resurrection Narrative has
been composed in the interest of faith and under the
influence of devout imagination. The Easter story of
Mark is unfortunately only a fragment; for the episode
of the women at the grave (xvi. 1–8) must originally
have been followed by an account of some appearance
of Jesus to Peter (and to the other disciples) in Galilee.
This ending has been lost, and much later a substitute
was supplied (xvi. 9–20) in some of the manuscripts.
Matthew and Luke have a series of Resurrection Narratives, and if one adds those given in John, it will be
clear how active the Christian imagination has been.[2]

The influence of the 'faith interest' or the 'cultic'
motive may also be seen in the manner in which even

in Mark the last meal of Jesus is narrated, i.e. in the same manner in which it was customary to celebrate the Lord's Supper in many Christian communities (Mark xiv. 22–25; cf. I Cor. xi. 23–25). The participant in the Supper shared in Jesus' Body and Blood, and thereby in his death and resurrection; and so it was natural to refer this meal back to the last meal of Jesus with his disciples before the Passion. The observance of the Supper was thought to have had its origin in the life of the Lord, and so the narrative of Jesus' Last Supper comes to be transformed into a 'cult-legend.' This motive, viz. to trace the origin of the 'cultic' observance in the fate of the cult-deity, may also be seen at work in other religions; the difference is that there the career of the deity is purely mythical, while the Christian cult-legend has real contacts with the life of Jesus.

The same is true of the Baptismal Narrative. Jesus was undoubtedly baptized by John the Baptist, a fact which involved difficulty from the Christian point of view as may be seen from Matthew iii. 14–15: Jesus ought not really to have submitted to the baptism of repentance; but he did so in order 'to fulfil all righteousness.' Later Christian writers have conceived the Baptismal Narrative as a cult-legend: in the baptism of Jesus our baptism has its basis and justification. Somewhat different is the conception of the Baptismal Narrative as given in Mark i. 9–11: it narrates Jesus' baptism as his vocation and anointing as Messianic King. By placing this narrative at the beginning of Jesus' ministry, Mark shows that the event is not to be

understood as a human but as a miraculous one. At
first the belief of the primitive community in Jesus as
the Messiah meant this: Jesus became the divinely ap-
pointed Messiah at his resurrection, and he will come
in the future, bringing salvation. Gradually, however,
his earthly life came to be viewed as the life and work
of the Messiah — at first with the reservation, that
his Messiahship remained a secret during this period.
Hence there lies over the account of Mark the veil of
the Messianic secret. It was only the demons who
recognized Jesus as Messiah; but they were commanded
to be silent. Later on, after Peter (by divine revelation, as Matthew xvi. 17 expressly says) had arrived at
the conviction of Jesus' Messiahship, the Master dis-
closed his Messianic destiny, privately to his disciples
(Mark viii. 27–33). Only on one occasion, and then
only for the three confidants, is the veil completely
lifted, and on the mount they behold for an instant
Jesus transfigured in heavenly glory (Mark ix. 2–8).
But they are forbidden to say anything about it until
after the resurrection (Mark ix. 9). This Transfiguration Narrative, probably originally one of the resurrection stories, shows clearly the way in which legends
created by faith influenced the narrative and gave to it
their own peculiar character.

Among such legends belongs also the scene of Peter's
confession (Mark viii. 27–33), and certainly its continuation in Matthew xvi. 17–19. This also is probably
a Resurrection Narrative which has been dated back
into the Life of Jesus. Another such legend is the nar-

rative of the Temptation of Jesus found in Mark (i. 12–13) and in Q (Matt. iv. 1–11 = Luke iv. 1–12), in which Jesus proves himself victorious over the devil and so points out the way to his followers in their struggle with Satan, and likewise gives them the assurance of victory. Legend has also colored the narrative of the entry of Jesus into Jerusalem, by representing it as the fulfilment of prophecy (Zechariah ix. 9): the Messiah was to make his entrance riding upon an ass.

The later evangelists add further legendary features, e.g. the story of Peter's miraculous draught of fish (Luke v. 1–11) and of his attempt to walk on the water (Matt. xiv. 28–32). Just as Matthew and Luke scarcely retain the Messianic secret, with which Mark has interwoven the life of Jesus, so these evangelists view the birth of Jesus as a miraculous event which in turn is accompanied by still other marvels, such as the announcement to the shepherds (Luke ii. 8–20) and the star which guided the Magi from the East to the Babe Jesus (Matt. ii. 1–12). A variety of motives derived from the Jewish Messianic hope and from Hellenistic beliefs in a Saviour God were at work in the creation of such legends, though we cannot here describe them in detail.

The gospel as a literary type was created, as far as we can see, by Mark, or at any rate was made use of by him; at the hands of Matthew and Luke, however, this becomes modified, since each is endeavoring to include as much as possible of the traditional material. It is for this reason that they combined Q (i.e. the Sayings-

source) with Mark. For this reason likewise the representation of Jesus as the teacher is much more greatly
emphasized than by Mark. They have also stressed the
miraculous character of the life of Jesus, since, as we
have seen, the legends are much more fully developed
than in Mark. This feature is still further emphasized
by Matthew, who intertwines numerous Old Testament
citations with the narrative, designed to show how the
life of the Messiah fulfilled ancient prophecy. Luke
betrays the effort to write as a historian and to find
points of contact for his narrative in various world-
historical dates (i. 5; ii. 1–3; iii. 1–2). Yet this is not
really based upon a genuine historical interest, but is
only the endeavor to bring home to educated Gentiles
the universal significance of the gospel story. In John
the original meaning of the gospel comes out in fullest
clarity, in that the evangelist while making free use of
the tradition creates the figure of Jesus entirely from
faith.

All this goes to show that the interest of the gospels
is absolutely different from that of the modern historian. The historian can make progress toward the recovery of the life of Jesus only through the process of
critical analysis. The gospels, on the other hand, proclaim Jesus Christ, and were meant to be read as
proclamations.

CHAPTER VII

RESULTS: OUR KNOWLEDGE OF THE HISTORICAL JESUS

What then is the final solution of the three involved problems described above (pp. 23f.): the Messianic consciousness of Jesus, the outward course of his life (and especially the grounds of his condemnation), and the relation between his eschatological and his ethical message?

Regarding the origin and development of his Messianic consciousness, we are, generally speaking, unable to say anything definite. Indeed, it must remain questionable whether Jesus regarded himself as Messiah at all, and did not rather first become Messiah in the faith of the community. The majority of scholars remain convinced of the first alternative. To me it appears rather that the second is the necessary consequence of the analysis of his words. At any rate, one may clearly see that Jesus did not come forward with the claims which from the Jewish point of view the Messianic title involved, but rather that his ministry was rightly characterized when it was said he was a prophet. Nevertheless, the movement which he inaugurated among the Jewish people may, and really must, be described as a Messianic movement, since it was carried on with the conviction that the Messianic prophecies were about to be fulfilled, that the Kingdom of God was about to ap-

pear, and that the signs of its arrival were to be seen
in the mighty works of Jesus, chiefly in the banishment
of the evil spirits. To those who stood outside it, this
movement must have appeared like any of the other
Messianic movements which in those decades convulsed
the Jewish people and finally led to the war with Rome
and the destruction of Jerusalem. The Roman procura-
tors suppressed such movements with blood, and Jesus
fell a victim to the intervention of the procurator Pilate.
As he came up to Jerusalem with his followers his arrival was viewed by the procurator as politically danger-
ous. Whatever part the Jewish authorities took therein
cannot now be made out, since the Passion Narrative is
too thickly overgrown with legend. For the later Christians the real enemies were the Jews; since they were
found to be their standing enemies and accusers, in the
work of the Christian mission (note the representation
in the Book of Acts), they were also made responsible
for the death of Jesus. It is, of course, possible that the
Jewish court in Jerusalem, in order to demonstrate its
own political innocence, had some part in the tragedy;
but at all events we are not entitled to assume that
Jesus' ethical teaching so roused the Pharisees and
scribes against him that he finally fell victim to their
enmity. That the steady opposition of the Pharisees
and scribes rests upon the artificial and schematic conception of later Christians has already been shown
(pp. 34f.).[1]

The most important question is that concerning the
content of Jesus' preaching. The investigation has
shown that both the eschatological and the ethical

teaching of Jesus belong equally to the oldest stratum of
the tradition, so that one can hardly call either one of
them secondary. Nor can we view the ethical precepts
of Jesus as 'interim-ethic' (see p. 24); for his demands
have an absolute character, and are by no means influenced in their formulation by the thought that the
end of the world is near at hand. Consequently, both
sides of the message of Jesus, the eschatological and the
ethical, must be conceived as belonging together. Did
Jesus preach the new ethics simply as a condition of
entrance into the Kingdom of God? In form this is
certainly true again and again; and yet this would be
no real union of the two elements, but only a superficial
and external relation, which, precisely in view of the
earnestness of his moral demands, would be hard to
conceive. Or is the announcement of the coming Reign
of God only the mythological or symbolical form, in
which he set forth his general faith in God as the Judge
and Rewarder? One can scarcely combine this with
the moral earnestness of his prophetic mission.

We must probably conclude that in the eschatological
as in the ethical teaching of Jesus the same fundamental
view of God and of man is presupposed. The eschatological expectation arose out of the conviction that God
is the final Reality, before whom everything earthly
fades away, and before whom man in his unworthiness
and worthlessness sinks to nothing. Only the future,
which is God's, can bring salvation to man; and this
future still faces man, in the present, and requires of
him the decision for the world or for God. This is
exactly the sense that Jesus' moral demands held. Jesus

sets forth neither an individual nor a social ethics; that
is, he measured the deeds of men neither according to
an ideal conception of human personality nor of human
society, but he taught men that the present instant is
the moment of decision, in which it is possible to yield
up every claim of one's own and submit obediently to
the will of God. It is this way of the good will, that
Jesus preached, which leads man directly to the awareness of his own unworthiness and worthlessness in the
sight of God, and of his own situation as faced with inevitable decision; it is only here that he learns the pro-
foundest meaning of God's forgiveness, which one can
receive only as a little child.

NOTES

FOREWORD

[1] Martin Albertz, *Die Synoptischen Streitgespräche,* 1921, p. v.
[2] New York, 1933; new revised and enlarged edition, 1957.

CHAPTER I

[1] There are a number of these synopses which offer the Greek text:
the most practical is that of A. Huck (7th ed., 1928); there is also a
Greek-German one, *The Four Gospels* by W. Larfeld (1911); and a German one by A. Huck (1908, second edition, 1928). [Huck's edition of
the Greek text is in general use even outside Germany. His text is that
of Tischendorf, in the main, as this text was preferred by H. J. Holtzmann, the author of the Commentary on the Synoptic Gospels which
Huck's volume was originally intended to accompany. There is a good edition with up-to-date critical apparatus and subheads in English, prepared by
F. L. Cross, Tübingen, 1936. This edition bears the title, *A Synopsis of
the First Three Gospels,* and a parallel volume, using the Revised Standard
Version of the New Testament for its text, but following exactly the arrangement and order and even numbering of sections in Huck, has been
prepared by Burton H. Throckmorton, Jr. (2d ed., New York, 1957).
This work is entitled, *Gospel Parallels: A Synopsis of the First Three
Gospels.*]

CHAPTER V

[1] German translation by Wieland. [A good modern English translation is that of Harmon in Vol. III of the Loeb Library edition. It is also translated in Vol. III of the Oxford translation by H. W. and F. G. Fowler. Reference should also be made to *Experience with the Supernatural in Early Christian Times,* by Shirley Jackson Case, 1929.]

[2] These examples are taken from U. von Wilamowitz-Moellendorf, *Griechisches Lesebuch* I, 1910, pp. 35–42.

[3] Volume I in the third edition, Volume II in the second edition, 1910; for lay readers the little work by H. Weinel is to be recommended: *Die Gleichnisse Jesu,* 4th edition, 1918.

[4] A number of rabbinic parables in German translation have been collected by P. Fiebig in his two volumes, *Ancient Jewish Parables* (*Altjüdische Gleichnisse*), 1904; *The Parables of Jesus* (*Die Gleichnisreden Jesu*), 1912. Fiebig's judgment is not infallible, and his polemic against Jülicher is quite perverse.

[5] G. Kittel, *The Problems of Palestinian Judaism and Primitive Christianity,* 1926. In addition to this instructive book, see also the great *Commentary on the New Testament from Talmud and Midrash* by Strack and Billerbeck, in the first two volumes of which (1922 and 1924) the Jewish parallels to the words of Jesus are given in great fulness.

[Readers unfamiliar with German will find relevant material in the *Commentary on the Synoptic Gospels* by C. G. Montefiore (two vols., 2nd edition, 1927) and in the same author's *Rabbinic Literature and Gospel Teachings* (1930); also in *Studies in Pharisaism and the Gospels* by I. Abrahams (two series, 1917 and 1924); in *Judaism in the First Centuries of the Christian Era,* by the late George Foot Moore (two vols., 1927. Vol. III, *Notes,* 1930); and also in *Jesus of Nazareth* by Joseph Klausner (Eng. tr., 1925).]

CHAPTER VI

[1] See the book by G. Bertram noted above on p. 30.
[2] See the book by L. Brun referred to on p. 31.

CHAPTER VII

[1] [See also *Jesus and the Pharisees: A Study in Christian Tradition,* by Donald W. Riddle (Chicago, 1928); H. Lietzmann, *Der Prozess Jesu* (Sonderausgabe aus den Sitzungsberichten der Preussischen Akademie der Wissenschaften, Phil.-hist. Klasse, 1931 [xiv]); the same author's article, 'Bemerkungen zum Prozess Jesu,' I and II, in *Zeitschrift f. d. Neutest. Wissenschaft,* xxx (1931), pp. 211–215, and xxxi (1932), pp. 78–84. In the same journal have appeared other articles on the subject, occasioned by Lietzmann's important discussion: M. Dibelius, 'Das historische

Problem der Leidensgeschichte' (xxx. 193–201); F. Büchsel, 'Die Blut-
gerichtsbarkeit des Synedrions' (xxx. 202–210); M. Goguel, 'A propos du
procès de Jésus' (xxxi. 289–301).]

PART TWO

PRIMITIVE CHRISTIANITY IN THE LIGHT OF GOSPEL RESEARCH

By Karl Kundsin

FOREWORD

Many a student of the New Testament and of Early Church History has felt with keen regret the lack of adequate sources for the earliest period of the church's long history. Walter Pater described the dark passage from the end of the first century to the end of the second as the church's 'subterranean age'; but an earlier period from the Resurrection to the Missionary Journeys of St. Paul, and, for the Palestinian church, from the Resurrection to the war under Hadrian, and even beyond, is almost equally obscure. True, the Book of Acts contains a number of traditions from this period; but they are few and brief, and they have been edited from a later point of view.

It is one special merit of Form criticism, the new German method of New Testament research, that it is not exclusively nor even primarily a study of literary development, but throws light upon the social and religious *milieu* in which the early traditions were handed down. This applies chiefly to the traditions contained in the Gospels, and the inquiry concerns those who preserved, selected, told and retold, and eventually wrote down the evangelic sayings, parables and narratives. In the present volume, Professor Kundsin of Riga has sketched the results of the application of the Form-critical method to the evangelic traditions. The volume shows how our knowledge of the earliest

Palestinian church, its outlook and aims, is widened by a careful study of the traditions which it handed down. The Gospels themselves become thus a source, or rather a collection of varied source-materials, not only for the life of Jesus but also for the early church. Incidentally, their place in the development of Christian thought and belief, and the general trustworthiness of their contents — thus answering an old question, but a persistent one — become much clearer.

The volume before us appeared in 1929 from the well-known press of Alfred Töpelmann in Giessen, and formed the second in the series initiated by Professor Bultmann's *Erforschung,* herewith translated. Taken together, the two companion works present an admirably brief and clear exposition of the main principles and leading results of Form criticism.

F. C. G.

CHAPTER VIII

THE POINT OF DEPARTURE

A vast amount of industry has been devoted, through a number of successive generations, to the investigation of the Gospels as historical sources. The chief aim of this scholarly research has been the recovery of the life-work and person of Jesus with the help of modern historical science. Complete success in the pursuit of this aim has not hitherto been achieved. Instead, there prevails at the present time a general conviction that the source-material contained in the gospels is insufficient for the drawing of a simple and more or less complete picture of the life of Jesus. Accordingly, it may appear that the labor of decades in this field has gone for nothing. But such a conclusion would surely be premature. Moreover, the situation is such that quite apart from important details relating to the person of Jesus, research has had other positive results, on another plane. In the hands of scholars, it has become increasingly clear that the gospels and their sources are primarily the expression and reflection of the faith and life of the early Christian churches which produced them. This is especially true of the fundamental elements in the Synoptic Gospels, or better, in the so-called Synoptic tradition, i.e. chiefly the so-called Logia or Sayings source (Q), and the basic material in the Gospel of Mark; but it is also true of the special material contained in Matthew and Luke. These various elements in the tradition may be understood in their full significance only when viewed primarily as the expression of the common life of the first Christians.

The recognition of this fact naturally provides a number of important new points of view for research. Before drawing conclusions regarding the person and work of Jesus, the Synoptic tradition (nothing will be said here concerning the Johannine tradition) must be evaluated as a source for the history of the early church. We may begin by sketching briefly the application of this point of view as seen in certain recent works. How, it may be asked, have these points of view fared in modern research?

There are three outstanding historical works dealing with the beginnings of Christianity which have been produced in recent years. Foremost among them is the book, *Primitive Christianity* (*Das Urchristentum*) by Johannes Weiss, which completed the life-work of that gifted scholar and was finished after his death by Rudolf Knopf (Göttingen, 1917). Another is the three-volume work of the historian Eduard Meyer, *The Origin and Early History of Christianity* (*Ursprung und Anfänge des Christentums;* Berlin, 1921–23). Finally, there is the series by a group of English and American scholars, entitled *The Beginnings of Christianity,* Part I, *The Acts of the Apostles,* edited by F. J. Foakes Jackson and Kirsopp Lake (London and New York, 1920–33).

Of these works that of Meyer is the least influenced by recent gospel research, and its account of the development of the primitive Christian community remains entirely under the influence of the idealized and retouched presentation of the Acts of the Apostles. Much greater emphasis has been placed upon the influence of the church tradition by both J. Weiss and Jackson and Lake. In particular they attempt, on important points, to supplement and to correct the account given in the Acts of the Apostles by making use of parts of the Palestinian tradition. Even here, however, other purposes have affected the account to such a degree that a thorough application of the new historical method has not yet been made, viz. the study of the origin and development of the tradition.

It may, therefore, be worth while even in this brief compass to make a modest attempt, setting aside every other point of view, to let the Synoptic tradition tell us its own story of the faith and life of the primitive Christian church, without asking what the Book of Acts has to say on this or that point, or how the story is to be worked into the general outline of contemporaneous history. Data derived from other sources must certainly be taken into account, however, where it is a question of the meaning or the relevance of one or another element in the tradition.

The point of departure for our study is the recognition of the successive and contiguous levels of development or growth in the Synoptic tradition. These are chiefly the following:

1. The oldest discoverable level of tradition, represented by the so-called Logia source (Q) and the oldest elements in the Gospel of Mark.

2. The earliest working over of selected traditional material, in the interests of the universalistic outlook of Hellenistic Christianity by Mark.

3. The revision and expansion of traditional material, from the ecclesiastical and legalistic point of view, in the Gospel of Matthew.

4. The later formulation of material in the Gospel of Luke, with its strong Hellenistic-Gentile sympathies.

From a comparison of the related levels numbered two and four, it appears that the process of development has passed through the following stages:

a. The earliest Palestinian stage, recoverable chiefly in Q and Mark.

b. The transition to a type of Gentile Christianity which was free from the Law and more open to the world, seen in Mark and in the special material of Luke.

c. The later Palestinian-Syrian stage in the development of ecclesiastical doctrine and organization, found in Matthew.

That the classification of the various elements in the tradition by their different levels cannot be carried through mechanically will be recognized by everyone who is even slightly familiar with the growth of living tradition, though it will receive further confirmation as our study proceeds.

The manner in which we shall undertake to carry through this method is best seen in Wilhelm Bousset's pioneer work, *Kyrios Christos,* the history of the faith in Christ from the beginnings of Christianity to Irenaeus (*Kyrios Christos, Geschichte des Christusglaubens von den Anfängen des Christentums bis Irenäus,* Göttingen, 1913, 2d ed., 1921). Special problems relating to the growth and literary formulation of the tradition are dealt with — among the more recent works — particularly in Rudolf Bultmann's *History of the Synoptic Tradition* (*Geschichte der Synoptischen Tradition,* Göttingen, 1921, 2d ed., 1931), and in Burnett Hillman Streeter's *The Four Gospels* (London, 1924; 2d ed., 1926; 4th impression, 1931).

CHAPTER IX

TRADITION AND CHURCH LIFE

Before we proceed to work out the separate stages, it should be pointed out that it was the fellowship in faith of the first Christians which provided the constructive factor in the tradition. One must be on his guard, in studying the Synoptic sources, against the tendency to view the origin of these sources more or less in accordance with literary procedure at the present day, when the producers are individual literary personalities. In the development of the gospels this was true only in a very limited measure. A careful examination of their history discloses that the selection, formulation, interpretation and, in part, likewise the arrangement of the material took place within the religious community and was carried on in steady contact with its life. This is absolutely certain in the case of those sections which have already been classified as relating to the community (*Gemeindestücke*). An instructive example is to be seen in the eighteenth chapter of the Gospel of Matthew, where single sayings of Jesus have been brought together and combined with the more developed expressions of the spirit of the community and with regulations borrowed from the Jewish Synagogue; these have been worked into a unity, in which a series of points of view reflecting the life of the church is to be found:

1. The position of importance assigned to the lowly and humble (vv. 1–5).
2. Unsparing condemnation of false leaders (vv. 6–9).
3. The duty of winning back the lost (vv. 10–14).
4. The method to be followed in recovering those who are in error, through the application of community discipline (vv. 15–20).
5. Unlimited readiness to forgive even repeated offences (vv. 21–33).

Not only these so-called 'community sections,' but even the purely narrative parts of the gospels were often formulated with a view to the actual problems of the common Christian life. Thus, for example, we have in Mark x. 2–27, in the form of a series of episodes from the life of Jesus — unquestionably arranged in a subject sequence — a treatment of several themes: the attitude of Christians to marriage, to children, to earthly possessions; and the series is concluded with the thoroughly characteristic summary found in x. 28–31. When one's eye has been trained to recognize such facts, it will be seen that there is hardly a passage (with the exception of certain parts of the Gospel of Luke) where this is not the case. Whether the evangelist is dealing with counsels regarding prayer, alms-giving and fasting, or with the attitude toward the Sabbath and the laws regarding ceremonial purity, or with concern for earthly treasure, or with the hostile world and with tribulation and persecution, it is the Christian fel-

lowship of the Church which is always to be seen in
the background, a fellowship bound together by a common experience and a common hope.

This may be made more clear by examining a few
important passages. 1. The Lord's Prayer as given in
the gospels is a prayer of the Christian community. It
has come down to us in two versions: Matthew vi.
9-15 and Luke xi. 1-4. The question, whether the
evangelists took it directly from the church's common
use or whether it reached them by way of the Sayings
collection, need not here be decided; the former alternative seems on the whole the more probable. The main
differences between the two recensions are as follows:
a different wording in the address — the now generally
used longer form is found in Matthew, the briefer
'Father' in Luke; the prayer for the gift of the cleansing power of the Holy Spirit in the older forms of the
text of Luke instead of the hallowing of the Name in
Matthew; the absence of the so-called third petition
('Thy will be done . . .') in Luke; the absence of the
final petition (for deliverance from evil) and of the
doxology in Luke (the latter likewise not found in any
of the older authorities for the text of Matthew). In
spite of these differences — we have mentioned only the
most important — the appropriateness of the Prayer for
use in the church is equally obvious in both forms (it
has been suggested that the Matthaean version was used
regularly at public worship, while that in Luke was
more appropriate for use at the service of Baptism).
In the case of Matthew's version this is most clearly ob-

servable in the introductory sayings: 'When ye pray, be not as the hypocrites. . . . When ye pray, use not vain repetitions like the Gentiles. . . . Be ye not like unto them, for your Father knoweth what things ye have need of. . . . But when ye pray say. . . . ' (Matt. vi. 5, 7, 9). Who are these persons addressed as 'ye,' as understood by the readers? It can only be the readers themselves, the believers in Christ, conscious of their separation from both Pharisees and Gentiles. Similarly in Luke, in spite of the entirely different introduction (xi. 1f), apparently presupposing a particular situation in the life of Jesus, the same holds true, with this sole difference that the need for a fixed form of Christian prayer is explained by reference to the prayer of the disciples of John the Baptist.

The Prayer itself bears out this observation. In Matthew the solemn address, 'Our Father . . .', is followed by seven liturgically arranged strophes, the first three of them characterized by their relation to God and the thought of his glory — *Thy* Name, *Thy* Kingdom, *Thy* Will; while the last four petitions relate to human needs — Give *us our* bread, forgive *us our* debts as *we* also have forgiven *our* debtors, lead *us* not into temptation, deliver *us* from evil. Whence comes this eightfold use of 'us' and 'our'? Even in the form in which we have the Prayer in the gospels, it is without doubt derived from the praying community. It has long been felt that the so-called fifth petition — for forgiveness of debts — was not really appropriate on the lips of Jesus. How understandable, on the contrary, does it become when the picture of the church sweeps into our vision! We see before us a fellowship of brothers, who look away from the earthly privations in the midst of which they find themselves to the coming Kingdom, the final glorification of the will of God, and who are inspired by the thought that they have been freed by God from sin and are now in a state of grace, strengthened to meet the last great trial (*peirasmos*) when the hour of everlasting decision arrives. Unreserved brotherly agreement with all one's fellow believers — 'as we also have forgiven '— which every disciple has made (either upon admission to the fellowship, or, repeatedly, at the beginning of each new service of worship; both interpretations are possible) is the obvious condition upon which God's forgiveness may be sought.

Though the features of the common life are fainter as we see them reflected in the Gospel of Luke, nevertheless here also it is a group of disciples who pray for the bestowal of the Spirit, the creative power of the new life, and are united by the thought of the daily bread provided for the hungry (or perhaps the heavenly food bestowed upon those who were awaiting the Kingdom?) and of the forgiveness of sins and of their common destiny, both temporal and eternal.

2. The Sermon on the Mount (Matt. v–vii) and its shorter parallel in Luke (vi. 20–48) was viewed as a program for the common life of Christians. What has just been said of the Lord's Prayer applies likewise to the inaugural address of Jesus in the gospels, which we call 'the Sermon on the Mount.'

Both Matthew and Luke provide the sermon with an introductory setting. The occasion is the gathering of a multitude from Galilee and the surrounding regions, or from the whole Jewish territory and the Syrian coast (cf. Matt. iv. 23ff; Luke vi. 17ff), who come to Jesus desirous of instruction and healing. Consequently, one expects in the contents of the address a corresponding attention to the character and the spiritual condition of this varied audience, especially since according to Matthew the multitude was strongly moved by the teaching it contains (Matt. vii. 28ff). However, if one analyzes the contents, it becomes clear at once that only a relatively small part of it was appropriate for such an audience: perhaps the first group of the Beatitudes, a few sayings regarding the objectionableness of personal judgments, regarding charity and forgiveness, probably also the sayings regarding the impermanence of wealth and the words of assurance regarding the loving care of the heavenly Father for his children — in brief, sayings which in their generality and ideality contain a message for everyone who is 'weary and heavy laden.' By no means, however, could this audience, representing various strata in the population, apply to themselves the words regarding the salt of the earth, the light of the world, the city set upon a hill, or — even less appropriately still — the designation 'persecuted for the sake of' Jesus (Matt. v. 11; Luke vi. 22) or the saying, 'Not everyone that saith unto me, Lord, Lord' (Matt. vii. 21f). The same applies to the counsel to enter through the narrow gate, and likewise

also to the new interpretation of the Law found in Matthew, which equally with the directions regarding true
alms-giving, prayer and fasting presuppose a clear separation from the surrounding world and the existence of
a new, distinct, social organization. It is, accordingly,
no accident that Matthew, in order to justify the contents of the sermon, brings in the smaller group of the
disciples, in addition to the multitude (v. 1f); while
Luke ignores these limitations and speaks of the ' great
crowd of disciples' (vi. 17). Quite naturally the reader
does not understand these to be the ' first' disciples,
who, according to the narrative in the gospels, began
following Jesus at once, but in both cases ' the disciples '
in the sense of primitive Christianity, i.e. once more
the early Christian community. These have already
singled themselves out from the surrounding world as
a newly formed group, faced with hostility and persecution, consciously engaged in a contest of principles and
a standing controversy with the legalistic Pharisees, in
need of warning against false prophets and against an
empty religion of mere profession, and likewise in need
of firm principles governing their own conduct, and
of general rules for the control of their social life in its
various forms. Thus we have here an example of the
interpretation and application of the sayings of the
Lord to the needs of the community.

3. Finally, the same observation may be made regarding the so-called ' Controversies,' and in an especially interesting way. It is chiefly the Gospel of
Mark that presents us with a whole series of passages be-

longing to this literary type. They are all more or less
the same in structure. A specified incident in the life
of Jesus arouses the displeasure of the official guardians
of the Law. The latter express themselves in caustic
remarks, which are intended to discredit the conduct
of Jesus or of his disciples in the eyes of those who are
present. Then follows either a counter-question by
Jesus, which his opponents cannot answer, or else a
decisive, penetrating saying of the Master which sets
the question in an entirely new light. This is true of
the question regarding fasting, the question of Sabbath-
desecration, the question of levitical purifications, the
tribute money, and others. Of course, one cannot doubt
that Jesus often came into collisions of this kind with
his Pharisaic neighbors. But it is very interesting to
observe (as Bultmann has done in his *Synoptic Tradition*) that in the respective narratives it is often not
Jesus himself who is charged with infringement of
rules, but rather his disciples. It is they who disregard
the practice of fasting (Mark ii. 18), who pluck the
grain on the Sabbath (Mark ii. 23), who eat bread with
unwashed hands, thereby breaking the Pharisaic rules
of purity (Mark vii. 1f). And even where it is the
Master himself whose conduct has aroused their displeasure, as, for example, in his intercourse with the
publicans, here again it is the disciples to whom the
complaint is made (e.g. Mark ii. 16). From all this it
is quite clear where the special interest in the Controversies contained in the gospels took its root: it is once
more the later community faced with its wholly con-

crete conditions of existence and its needs, which stands
behind the tradition and in the Controversies found
its weapons for use in the struggle with the Jewish
opposition.

This leads us finally to an observation which is of the
greatest importance in determining the age and the
origin of the tradition, the fact, namely, that the earliest
phase of the common tradition presupposes the land
and the speech of *Palestine,* and carries us back to the
period before the destruction of the Holy City by Titus.
The most pertinent discussion, in support of these facts,
is still to be found in Julius Wellhausen's *Introduction
to the Three Synoptic Gospels* (*Einleitung in die Drei
Synoptischen Evangelien,* Berlin, 2d ed. 1911) and in
his *Commentaries on the Gospels.* We may refer to the
well-known passage in Matthew v. 21f with its Aramaic
epithets, which are still retained in the Greek text, and
its reference to Palestinian court procedure. Further,
in Matthew v. 23 the temple in Jerusalem is presupposed
as still in existence; it is also quite clear that it can easily
be reached by the members of the community. The
city of Jerusalem as the center of the Christian church
seems to be taken for granted likewise in Matthew x.
23. On the other hand, the conditions out in the province, with its flat country, are clearly reflected in the
Mission of the Disciples, Matthew x. 5ff and parallels.
The characteristic Semitic form of greeting, ' Peace be
with you,' maintained itself in Greek translation, where
its original sense, as the text shows, became the basis
for a further development of its meaning (cf. Luke x. 5;

Matt. x. 12f). An interchange of the ideas of 'cleansing' and 'giving alms,' which was possible only in Aramaic (in which the words sound alike), is presupposed by the two variants of the saying in Luke xi. 41 and Matthew xxiii. 26 — where the wording of Matthew gives the correct meaning. Examples might easily be multiplied to show the Aramaic basis both of sayings in Q and passages in Mark. We may refer to the well-known Aramaisms, 'Rabbi' and 'Abba.' From all this it is obvious that a considerable part of the tradition was derived from the Aramaic-speaking Palestinian community, and, in fact, partly from the Jerusalem, partly from the provincial groups. The self-designation of the members of the community is *adelphoi,* i.e. brothers. The highest authority is that of 'the Twelve,' as spokesmen and leaders, and especially as the connecting link between the mass of Christians and the Master. There was a time when the theocratic prerogatives of the twelve were pictured with extraordinary realism (Matthew xix. 28; cf. Luke xxii. 30).

Thus we find a number of lines leading back from the Synoptic tradition to its true place of origin, the Palestinian church. No amount of private editorial revision was able to remove these traces. This justifies us in endeavoring to examine somewhat more closely the various strands of tradition, confident that we may still be able to feel the beating life-pulse of the earliest community.

CHAPTER X

THE PRIMITIVE PALESTINIAN CHURCH

I. The Doctrine of the Son of Man

The religious situation of the primitive Palestinian community, related backwards as it was to the message of Jesus and forwards to the faith of later Hellenistic Christianity, had its own special characteristics. It is best described, borrowing the phrase from the thesis of Bousset's *Kyrios Christos,* in the words, 'Son of Man faith' or 'Son of Man dogma.' At the basis of this faith lay the conviction that Jesus of Nazareth was 'the Son of man.' What did this signify? The meaning of the formula can be understood only by reference to the figure of the Son of Man found in contemporary Jewish and early Christian Apocalyptic (Daniel, the Book of Enoch, IV Ezra, Mark xiii., cf. Matt. xxiv). Judging from the evidence of this literature, we may conclude that 'the Son of Man' was a recognized figure in certain eschatological-apocalyptic circles, upon whom centered, in time of stress, the expectation of the visible coming of the Reign of God 'from above,' together with the destruction of the existing world-powers ('the four great beasts') who had opposed themselves to God. The faith in Jesus as the Son of Man meant accordingly the identification of the earthly person, Jesus of Nazareth, with the figure of the 'Heavenly Man' (*Son of*

96

Man in accordance with Semitic usage was equivalent to *Man*) at whose coming at the end of days the world-powers should disappear and the blessed Reign of God begin.

On the basis of the source material found in the Synoptic Gospels, where the term 'Son of Man' appears about thirty-seven times (not counting doublets) and where, indeed, the term is found almost exclusively in the mouth of Jesus himself, it seems possible, or rather even probable, that Jesus had already referred to himself as the Son of Man.   In no case, however, had he clearly and unambiguously identified himself with the Son of Man. This is evident from certain old sayings in which the Son of Man appears as a being of heavenly nature distinct from Jesus and in fact contrasted with him. For example, Mark viii. 38, cf. Luke ix. 26: 'For whosoever shall be ashamed of me and of my words, the Son of Man also shall be ashamed of him, when he cometh in the glory of his Father with the holy angels;' or Luke xii. 8: 'Everyone who shall confess me before men, him shall the Son of Man also confess before the angels of God.' The situation was quite different in the primitive community. A careful examination of the 'Son of Man sayings' shows that at a certain point, sometime after the appearances of the Risen Lord — apart from the Resurrection experiences there would naturally have been no such faith — the conviction arose and began its course: Jesus himself is the Son of Man. It was himself and none other whom he had designated by this cryptic expression. In other words,

he is the heavenly Messiah, by his very nature distinguished from all the mighty of the earth, at whose
coming the Kingdom of God, the new aeon, was to
appear in visible form, and whose Kingdom in contrast
to those of this earth was to be an everlasting one. By
this identification of Jesus with the Son of Man the
peculiarity of the Christian Messianic community as
distinct from other groups who expected the Messiah
or the coming of the new Age was clearly marked:
what the world had never dreamed of, is a fact; the
Messiah had already visited the world and tarried here
for a brief time unrecognized. The Jews in their blind-
ness had delivered him over to be crucified. Blessed
were they, whose eyes were open, who in the brief days
of his earthly life or in the narrow time of grace which
still remained confessed their faith in him! Woe to
them that had denied or rejected the one by whom the
destiny of mankind was to be determined!

The first Christians had much in common with the
surrounding world, i.e. with other religious communities and movements in Palestine, for example with the
disciples of John the Baptist: the expectation of the
speedy end of this world, and of the Judgment, the conviction of the necessity of a radical repentance, and so
on. The peculiar possession of the Christians was their
confidence that in the person of Jesus the heavenly
Messiah had already appeared and that thus they were
aware of the standards which would prevail at the Judgment. In contrast to the prevailing view, it was their
deepest conviction that this exalted, divine being had

manifested himself not in dominion over others but in lowly service (Mark x. 45f; cf. Luke xxii. 25ff). In his humiliation was found the necessary pre-condition to his exaltation: he *must* be rejected of men, suffer and die, in order in this way to enter his heavenly glory and be exalted as heavenly Messiah (Mark viii. 31; ix. 31; x. 33; cf. also Luke xxiv. 25f and Phil. ii. 5ff). Confession of this Son of Man, thus exalted through abasement, assured one a share in the future heavenly blessedness.

This was the form in which the primitive community conceived of God in the person of Jesus. In the deepest sense this meant the conviction that the secret of the divine nature, abasing itself in lowliness and enduring the undeserved sufferings of the humanity of Jesus, was made known as something different from and opposed to the ' world.' The heavenly being had appeared upon earth, but the world had not comprehended him.

This is the light in which all the Son of Man sayings in the gospels are to be interpreted. The term is thus to be understood when the title ' Son of Man ' is used with reference to the coming of Jesus in glory (in the eschatological passages), or when it accompanies the sayings regarding suffering and rejection at the hands of men (the second main group of sayings), or, finally, when it is introduced into passages which referred originally to the earthly person of Jesus or perhaps even to the genus ' man.'

While thus, on the one hand, a new understanding of the nature of God received expression, on the other it offered a rich opportunity for the introduction of old

pre-Christian and sub-Christian ideas into the common
faith. Here belongs the whole complex of eschatological-apocalyptic views, which had come to be associ-
ated with 'the Son of Man' in the Jewish-Oriental
eschatology: the reckoning of the years and days to
precede the coming of the end of the world, the doctrine
of the last 'great tribulation' and the signs in the sun,
moon and stars, the notion of the visible coming of
the Judge of the world upon the clouds of heaven, of the
resurrection of the dead and the last Judgment, the
picturing of the heavenly blessedness of the redeemed
and the eternal pains of the wicked. Many a section
in the gospels, chiefly the so-called Little Apocalypse
in Mark xiii with its parallels, witnesses to the way in
which these popular conceptions prevail and maintain
themselves. Words like those about the coming of the
Son of Man 'at the right hand of Power' (Mark xiv.
62) or of the coming of the end before the first generation should have died (Mark ix. 1), i.e. in the immediate
future (Matt. x. 23), were now placed in the mouth
of Jesus himself.

It was in this conception of 'thorough-going eschatology' that Albert Schweitzer supposed he had found
the heart of the message of Jesus — quite incorrectly,
we believe. The recognition of the coloring-over of
the original portrait as a result of the Son of Man
dogma of the primitive community warns us to be cau-
tious: it is not so much Jesus as the faith of the primitive
community which comes before us here and receives
characteristic expression.

II. THE NEW ATTITUDE TOWARD THE SURROUNDING WORLD AND TOWARD THE BRETHREN

This certainty of the near approach of the end of the world and of the coming of the Son of Man resulted in a definite attitude toward the surrounding world and toward the brethren. The attitude toward the world which we find in the primitive community is essentially the same as that which we learn from Paul: 'The time is shortened, that henceforth those that have wives may be as though they had none; and those that weep, as though they wept not; and those that rejoice, as though they rejoiced not; and those that buy, as though they possessed not; and those that use the world, as not using it to the full: for the fashion of this world passeth away' (I Cor. vii. 29ff). In other words, a serious view of the approaching end of the world resulted in a realization of the necessity of complete inner separation from the world, and likewise the most extreme concern for the salvation of the largest possible number of one's own people from the threatened destruction. It is true that fearless confession of Jesus as the Son of Man was, as we have seen, the first prerequisite to participation in the coming salvation (Matt. x. 32, 33, from Q; Mark viii. 38, etc.). Even John the Baptist became a warning example, since he had taken offense at the outward lowliness of the figure of Jesus (Matt. xi. 2ff). However, confession of Jesus was by no means to be a confession merely with the lips. Opposed to this stood the clear meaning of the saying: 'Not everyone that

saith unto me, Lord, Lord, shall enter into the Kingdom
of Heaven; but he that doeth the will of my Father who
is in heaven ' (Matt. vii. 21f; in briefer form, Luke vi.
46: ' Why call ye me, Lord, Lord, and do not the things
which I say?'). Another fragment of the tradition
relates that the decisive factor in the Judgment is to be
one's relation to the poor, the shelterless, the naked and
hungry, since ' Inasmuch as ye did it unto one of these
my brethren, even these least, ye did it unto me ' (Matt.
xxv. 40).

The picture that comes before us is that of a community of the lowly (*mikroi*), of brethren and sisters
who have nothing to lose in this world, since they have
completely detached themselves from all possessions.
As a matter of fact, the disciples upon leaving Galilee,
in order to form in Jerusalem the community of those
looking forward to the coming of the Kingdom, had
forsaken everything (cf. Mark x. 28ff = Matt. xix.
29 = Luke xviii. 28f), viz. house and land, brothers and
sisters, father and mother, in some cases even wife
(Luke) and child; i.e. they had for the most part abandoned not only their personal belongings, but even
house and home, inasmuch as these stood in the way of
complete devotion to the 'one thing necessary.' In
their own lives they had carried out the command to
give up the treasure which moth and rust corrupt, in
order to obtain a treasure in heaven (Matt. vi. 19f; cf.
Luke xii. 33f). They had themselves sold all that they
possessed in order to obtain the hidden treasure, the
pearl of great price (Matt. xiii. 44–45), and thus had

set themselves free from anxious care for the morrow, in accordance with the saying of Jesus (Matt. vi. 33; Luke xii. 31).

There were undoubtedly members of the community who had originally been well-to-do but who had sacrificed their property for the benefit of the poor (their fellow Christians), in order to become rich in the Kingdom of Heaven (cf. Luke xii. 33). Others had at first endeavored to live on with their unconverted relatives, until it became clear how impossible it is to live in two worlds, and they applied to themselves the saying of Jesus, 'I am not come to bring peace, but division' (Luke xii. 51).

All the more ardent was the devotion of such members to the new life of the brotherhood. The Son of Man himself had come in order to minister, and accordingly this was to be the very life of his disciples, who were not above their Master (Luke xxii. 25f). In counselling even the most menial tasks, e.g. at table, this was carried even to the extent of completely breaking down every distinction between high and low, young and old (Luke xxii. 27).

Impressive in the sincerity and humility of their conduct were those who gave evidence of their brotherly attitude in a literal fulfilment of the counsels of the Master, who showed their complete contempt for social customs by inviting as table guests not their social equals but the poor of the town or village (Luke xiv. 12ff) or, when they were themselves invited, by seating themselves in the lowest place (Luke xiv. 7ff).

Another characteristic note was the relation of the sexes. They were indeed far removed from the views of radically minded ascetic circles who looked upon marriage as sinful and required the separation of husband and wife. On the contrary, appealing to the Master, who had frequently taken the part of woman, who was at that time all but completely deprived of legal rights, they looked upon marriage as absolutely indissoluble. A double morality in marriage was simply not permitted (Mark x. 2ff): it was only later, when the moral purity of the early period had already suffered a decline (perhaps as a result of the revival once more of the rabbinic point of view), that exceptions began to be allowed, since the act of adultery rendered impossible a further continuance of marriage, according to human standards (note the clauses in the text of Matt. xix. 9 and v. 32, compared with Mark x. 11 and Luke xvi. 18). Nevertheless, there were certainly others who for the sake of purity avoided every contact with woman, and believed it possible to avoid even the thought of such contact. At any rate, this question arose fairly early, and it appears that from the beginning two different conceptions existed side by side. One may compare Matthew v. 28ff or Matthew xix. 10ff with the passage in Mark regarding divorce (Mark x. 2–12) and likewise, along with it the view of Paul in I Cor. vii.

Perhaps the most conspicuous note was the realization that in view of the nearness of the last great day, one must without delay come into agreement with all his adversaries, chiefly, of course, with those of his own fellowship. The duty of reconciliation and of forgiveness is set forth in a whole series of passages, frequently with an eschatological motivation (cf. Matt. v. 25f = Luke xii. 57–59; Matt. v. 24f; Matt. v. 43f, cf. Luke vi. 27f; Luke vi. 37; Matt. xviii. 21ff). Not a few, who had caused one another deep humiliation and the bitter sense of injustice or who had insisted upon revenge, were now, though living in various spheres of life, members of one and the same brotherhood. For this reason it was self-evident that all injustice and bitterness must be consigned to forgetfulness — first of all, of course, upon admission to the community. Only thus could the former enemies come into the presence of God and say the common prayer: 'Forgive us our debts as we have also forgiven our debtors.'

The fundamental motive in this attitude toward one another and toward the surrounding world is to be found in the awareness that one already belongs to another and better world, at least that one has been called to enter it. And that better world might arrive any day.

It was only natural that under such circumstances the eyes of many should turn repeatedly to that better world in which they hoped to receive the hundredfold reward for all the humiliations and deprivations they had suffered. And so it came to pass, especially in times when the power of the spirit grew weak, that, following a shift in the original point of view, according to which things heavenly were everything, the earthly nothing, the renunciation of the world and its good things was viewed as an achievement for which an eternal *reward* was at hand. Thus the moral principle of reward crept in time into the view of the community, as is reflected in many sayings in Q, e.g. Luke xiv. 14, 'For thou shalt be recompensed at the resurrection of the just,' or Luke vi. 23, cf. Matthew v. 12, 'Rejoice in that day, and leap for joy: for behold, your reward is great in heaven'; Matthew vi. 4, 7, 18: 'And thy Father who seeth in secret shall recompense thee,' etc. Here we may clearly see the influence of the older religious outlook, which for centuries had dominated popular thought and in Pharisaism had become a dogma.

When one had abandoned his earthly possessions he was readily inclined, in reliance on the word of the Master, to picture to himself the treasure which he should accordingly receive in the age to come. In exchange for the lost earthly family and relatives one hoped to be compensated through the fellowship of the blessed in the coming Kingdom (Matt. xix. 29, 30), and in place of shameful treatment in this world to receive a place in 'Abraham's bosom' (Luke xvi. 19–31). However, it must be pointed out that in comparison with the Pharisaic doctrine of reward the idea of recompense remained more or less on the periphery (expressed most clearly in the strongly Judaistic strata of the Gospel of Matthew); moreover, any tendency toward excessive expectation of reward would be checked by the words of the Master to the sons of Zebedee (Mark x. 35ff) and the parable of the Workers in the Vineyard (Matt. xx. 1ff) where the 'last' receive the same reward at the 'first.'

This inner separation from the world and its good things in order to be prepared for the life to come was nevertheless only one side of the attitude which the eschatological Son of Man faith produced in the disciples. In addition to the concern for personal salvation, there was also an ardent desire to convey this decisive knowledge to the surrounding world, first of all to their own people, so far as the Son of Man and his coming was still a secret to them. Thus the eschatological faith in the Son of Man led directly to the missionary activity of the primitive church.

We may infer from the missionary sayings and the missionary addresses of Mark and Q (cf. Mark vi. 6-11; Matt. x. 5-16; Luke ix. 1-5 and x. 2-12) that, contrary to the representation of the Book of Acts, Jerusalem was by no means the only headquarters of the Christian mission. The movement covered the entire country: from house to house, from village to village, from city to city went the missionaries with the message upon which the happiness of thousands depended. It was to this situation that the saying applied: 'Whatsoever ye have said in the dark shall be heard in the light; and what ye have spoken in the ear in the inner chambers shall be proclaimed upon the house-tops' (Matt. x. 27; cf. Luke xii. 3 and Mark iv. 21-23). It would seem as if at first the new message had been related only as a kind of secret to those within the circle of personal intimacy. This was true no doubt at the time when 'for fear of the Jews' the disciples gathered behind closed doors.

This earliest stage was soon followed by a second, since the message could no longer be restrained, but by inner necessity found its way to the public (to use the language of the Book of Acts — following Pentecost). The same thought, that the message must be released and made public, is found also in the saying about the light which does not belong under a bushel, and that other saying about the city set on a hill (Matt. v. 14ff; cf. Mark iv. 21; Luke viii. 16; xi. 33). The description of the wandering life of the missionaries has come down to us in several versions (Mark vi.; Luke ix. and x.; Matt. x.), all of which relate originally to conditions in Palestine. Mark, in contrast to the two other synoptists, permits the use of staff and sandals, and does not expressly forbid a second coat; he apparently wishes to modify and soften the impression of extreme simplicity, or indeed poverty, which the other accounts produce, since it was required by the taste of his readers or the conditions of his time. Even so a powerful impression remains. Without a penny of money, without any baggage whatsoever, without any certain promise of support and hospitality, these first messengers set about their task. Probably in imitation of a custom of the Master in sending his companions two by two on brief preaching tours, these missionaries went in pairs from village to village and city to city, beginning in private homes but soon proceeding to the public squares. It was the message of the nearness of the Kingdom, which they preached, and of Jesus who was about to return as the Son of Man.

The first wave of this missionary movement took place exclusively in Jewish territory. In view of the prohibition in Matthew x. 5 this is not to be identified with the later Samaritan mission (described in Acts viii. 4ff): 'Go not into any way of the Gentiles, and enter not into any city of the Samaritans.' This rule can have obtained only at the very earliest time, when the proclamation of the message to Israel was looked upon as the prerequisite to the coming of the Son of Man (cf. Matt. x. 23).[1] In more than one respect this picture contained in the gospels corrects the popular impression, based on the Book of Acts. The Mission was by no means confined to a few outstanding missionaries, who were 'apostles and evangelists,' charged with the duty of bearing the great Message leading to decision; rather it was the humble and the lowly, the 'little ones,' who neither were nor aimed to be prophets or public speakers in the grand style. It was to children in spirit and to the immature — to 'babes' — that God had revealed the mystery (Matt. xi. 25), who now for the first time appeared before the world, and often enough had no idea beforehand what they were to say, unless the 'Spirit of their Father' should come with help in the critical hour. This experience they never forgot (Matt. x. 20).

Thus the heroism of these people, soon to prove itself in hostility and persecution, was a heroism not of the great and the mighty, but of the humble. The hostile attitude of the scribes and rulers of the synagogue was already a threatening power, one that must have in-

spired fear and apprehension, not to mention the possible intervention of higher authorities (Matt. x. 17f).
Hence the to us apparently exaggerated warning: ' Behold, I send you forth as sheep in the midst of wolves '
(Matt. x. 16).

Greater than the danger, however, was their assurance. The worst that could happen to them, beyond the
persecution and insults and the humiliating corporal
punishments of the synagogue, was bodily death. But
what did this amount to contrasted with the possession
of the life beyond, of which no power in this world was
able to deprive them? Hence the thought contained
in the saying, ' Be not afraid of them that kill the body,
but are not able to kill the soul: but rather fear Him
who is able to destroy both soul and body ' (cf. Matt. x.
28; Luke xii. 4; from Q). The One, for whom the
sparrow was not too small to notice, will certainly be
able to keep them safe in their hour of need (Matt. x.
29; cf. Luke xii. 6). And though they were called upon
to endure much undeserved suffering, the thought all
but suggested itself that the slave was no better than his
Lord, nor the disciple than his Master (Matt. x. 24f).
Whoever refuses to take up his ' cross ' and follow Jesus,
is not worthy of him (Q and Mark).

III. THE ATTITUDE TOWARD JUDAISM, THE BEGINNINGS OF PUBLIC WORSHIP AND TEACHING

The prevalent idea, which supports itself chiefly by
appeal to St. Paul (especially Gal. ii.) but which may

also appeal to the Book of Acts (xii. 17; xxi. 17ff) and to some other later writers, is that the true head and spiritual leader of the Jerusalem or Palestinian churches during the second and third decades (excepting, perhaps, the earlier years) was James the Just, the Brother of the Lord. It has been customary to view him, in the light of the sources just named, as a strongly legalistic Jew, who never once thought of the separation and independence of the Christian community but maintained the 'Judaistic' point of view, that the Law and the religious worship of the Jews were without exception obligatory upon Christians. The fact of the existence of such a tendency and the position of leadership held by James in certain circles is far too well attested for us to disregard it. It is an error, however, to assume that the point of view and the authority of this Brother of the Lord was recognized throughout all of primitive Palestinian Christianity. The common tradition, which we find in the Synoptic Gospels, teaches us otherwise. Both in Mark and (especially) in Q, we find hardly a trace of this legalistic view of which James was the champion. The only clear references to the binding authority of the Law, for Christians, and of its exposition by the scribes, are found in the special material of the Gospel of Matthew. In this connection belongs the passage in Matthew v. 19–20, where the fulfilment even of the least commandments is required of Christians; and likewise the strange saying in Matthew xxiii. 2–3, where the teaching authority of the 'scribes and Pharisees' is apparently to be recognized by Christians. Prob-

ably Matthew xviii. 15ff likewise deserves to be con-
sidered in this connection, a passage in which the
organization of the local Christian church rests upon
an Old Testament, or rather a synagogal, basis. One
also thinks of the sayings in Matthew x. 5 and 23 with
their strong emphasis upon Jewish particularism.
Nevertheless, these expressions occupy but a compara-
tively insignificant place in the tradition and are for the
most part found exclusively in the peculiar matter of
one gospel, that of Matthew; so that one may perhaps
conclude that what we have here is only the last vestige
of the Jerusalem-Jacobite tradition.[2] It must not, however, be forgotten that even in these passages, as generally throughout the Synoptic tradition, there is not
the slightest trace of any preeminence assigned to James
the Brother of the Lord (indeed, the Gospel of Matthew is explicitly 'Petrine'). Thus we arrive at the
conclusion that the circle about James, whatever may
have been their importance in other respects, had little
to do with the formulation of the gospel tradition. The
really creative tradition-making life-center of the primitive community, as far as Palestine is concerned, was
certainly to be found outside this altogether too conservative and narrowly legalistic party. The real bearers of the genuinely world-conquering energy of the
new religion are to be sought in the groups forming the
provincial communities in Palestine, who in the midst
of constant hostility on the part of their neighbors preserved and maintained their peculiar characteristics.
When persecution broke out, it scarcely affected those

who were gathered about James (cf. Acts viii. 1; xxi. 1ff). The bearers of the living word at this time were, on the contrary, as Q makes clear in ample detail, those who were oppressed and persecuted.

In such circles the attitude toward the Law and toward Judaism, as a natural result of the fact of persecution, was an entirely different one. There was no consciousness of solidarity with Pharisaic scribism, but, on the contrary, a deep and fundamental cleavage, characteristic of the group. These Christians felt themselves much closer to the broad mass of the ' people of the land ' than to official Judaism — i.e. to the ' Am-ha-ares ' whom we know from rabbinic polemics, who, like those who handed down the tradition contained in Mark and Q, maintained a lax attitude toward the Law, disregarded the rules for ceremonial purity, and so on.

However, this by no means disproves the fact that the native soil even of this type of primitive Christian life was the theocratic, Old Testament, Jewish community. Against the explicit and commonly recognized sacred customs of the popular religion, rooted deep in the life of the people, there was no protest. The sacredness of the temple in Jerusalem and, with certain limitations (cf. the pericope of the temple-cleansing), even its cultus were recognized (compare at this point the saying in Matt. v. 23f — unless this really reflects the narrower conception of the followers of James, which to some extent has influenced the Gospel of Matthew). The Sabbath, since it was divinely ordained, retained its meaning as the chief day in the week and

the occasion for the assembling of the community for
worship and edification (note the appeal that is made to
the custom of Jesus who regularly on the Sabbath went
to the synagogue; and likewise the controversies in
Mark on the subject of healing on the Sabbath). We
may assume that similarly many other religious customs, e.g. the observance of the festivals, were preserved
among the Christians. The center of gravity and the
chief point of interest lay, however, for the group opposed by their Pharisaic neighbors, no longer in a common antiquity, which united them, but in the 'new
wine,' which the old skins could no longer contain. It
was already realized that the fulfilment of the Law in
the sense of Jesus' command of love (Mark xii. 28ff)
meant something radically new. For those who 'confessed' the Son of Man, for those who bore the cross,
the punctilious observance of rabbinic refinements in
the interpretation of the Law (the disregard of which
was also a charge against the Am-ha-ares) had completely lost meaning — such as the sanctifying of the
Sabbath, the observance of the Levitical rules of purity,
the tithing of one's income, the practice of fasting, and
many other details of the religious life as lived by strict
orthodox Jews. This fact is indisputably proved by the
amount of space given in the Palestinian strata of tradition to the Controversies over these matters (Mark ii.
18–22, 23–27; iii. 1–6; vii. 1–23), as also in the devastating polemic against the legalism of the Pharisees and
scribes, which, clearly Palestinian in form, is found in
the woes in Q (Luke xi. 37ff and xx. 46f; cf. Matt. xxiii.

4–36). Though naturally many of the outward forms of
Jewish life and thought persisted, as far as form went,
in the Palestinian community, they had lost much of
their meaning and become of secondary importance, as
belonging to this passing 'age.' Most important of all,
the life which clothed itself in these forms was new.
Not only in the synagogue but also in private houses,
the followers of the Messiah Jesus gathered for the up-
building of the fellowship in faith and love. Not only
did these gatherings take place on the Sabbath, but
sometimes even daily. Although the common public
worship followed the formal pattern of the synagogue
service, the attitude was nevertheless entirely different.
The leaders were no longer teachers of the Law, unap-
proachable in dignity, but simple 'brothers' chosen
from the congregation, not clad in long robes or gar-
ments of prayer, but in plain everyday apparel (Mark
xii. 38f; Matt. xxiii. 5; Luke xx. 46; cf. Matt. x. 10), not
infrequently — judged by outward appearance — the
lowliest of the lowly. Humility was their most impressive characteristic. Class distinctions no longer obtained. Even the customary Jewish forms of address to
a teacher, 'Rabbi' or 'Father,' were avoided. One was
their Master, Christ, and they had but one Father, God
(Matt. xxiii. 7–12). When they joined in prayer, it was
no longer to say the customary 'Shema' ('Hear, O Israel'), or the customary Seven-fold Sabbath Prayer, or
the long 'Eighteen-fold Prayer,' but rather the new
Seven-fold Prayer, the 'Our Father.' The customary
reading from the Scripture received a new significance,

and especially the exposition which followed it, since it served to make known the new interpretation of the Bible's meaning (cf. Luke iv. 17ff; xxiv. 25ff; Matt. v. 21ff). The center of interest lay in those Old Testament passages which were understood to refer to Jesus. Here was found the basis for the Christian 'Scripture-proofs' and for the comparison of the earthly life of Jesus with the Old Testament 'promises,' which were now set in a new light. This was especially true of passages in which were found predictions of the coming of the Messiah in lowly guise, his death, and his succeeding glorification. It is not surprising that not only such clear references as Isaiah ch. liii, but also passages like Zechariah ix. 9, xiii. 7, and scattered expressions in the Psalms which had to do with the undeserved suffering of the righteous (especially Psalms xxii and lxix), were literally referred to Jesus; in this manner many vivid touches were introduced into the Passion Narrative — such as the description of the Triumphal Entry into Jerusalem, the scattering of the disciples, the scene at the cross, and Jesus' last cry of dereliction.

To these gatherings was added a common meal which had cultic significance. This was inspired partly by memories of Jesus' own fellowship at meals with his disciples in Galilee, but probably was likewise an imitation of the Sabbath meal of the Jewish synagogue; compare the stories of the Feeding of the Multitude and the oldest account of the Last Supper of Jesus with his disciples, viz. that contained in Luke xxii. 15ff (according to the oldest and best text). The distribution of bread (and fish?) served at the same time to provide for the poor and needy, who formed a large part of the group. Through the cultic reference of the meal the custom naturally arose, at a specific moment, probably at the beginning, of consecrating the gifts of food with prayer and words of blessing, thus to remind the participants of the living bread which God had vouchsafed through his Servant, Jesus, to those who hungered and thirsted for eternal life in the coming Kingdom.[3]

In these common gatherings, which enabled the Christians more and more clearly to recognize the peculiar privileges which were theirs as distinguished from their neighbors, the saying of Jesus received an ever renewed and oft repeated fulfilment, and an ever deepening meaning: ' I thank thee, O Father, that thou didst hide these things from the wise . . . and didst reveal them unto babes ' (Matt. xi. 25; Luke x. 21), and with it that other: ' Unto you is given the mystery of the Kingdom of God; but unto them that are without, all things are done in parables' (Mark iv. 11).

It is an inevitable question, if we must not, in view of this peculiar consciousness of separation from the hostile and persecuting world, speak even thus early of a new ecclesiastical organization, distinct from the synagogue but parallel to it (Greek *ekklesia,* Aramaic *kenishta*). It is characteristic, however, of the earliest strands of tradition that this term was not yet in use. At first no need was felt for a fixed organization, with officers and cultic formulae. Even the rite of initiation and dedication of new converts, which was later traced back to the

institution of Jesus himself, viz. baptism in the Name of
Jesus, only gradually made its way to acceptance, as we
may see in tracing the growth of the tradition; it grew
up by analogy and likewise to a certain extent in contrast to ' the baptism of John,' a process in which the
accession of many members from the circle of John's
disciples must have been an influential factor. At first
the opposition to every kind of formal ablution was too
great.

At the same time, though specifically Christian forms
or regulations governing worship and organization
were lacking, there was already in existence, viewing it
in its essence, a new religious fellowship, which may
perhaps most appropriately be designated as the church
of ' latter day saints.' On account of their eschatological
view-point, external forms were entirely a matter of
indifference. On the other hand, emphasis was laid
upon the fact that the ' true ' Israel, Israel in accordance
with the divine idea, had been singled out, and as such
could rejoice in the inheritance of the Old Testament
promises. In the number twelve of the original apostles
was seen a significant confirmation of this idea (Matt.
xix. 28).

It was in their extraordinary moral earnestness and
their inner independence and fearlessness as they faced
the world, combined with ardent love for their Master,
that we find the strength of the new faith, as also in
their conception of the last things, a conception sus-
tained by contemporary apocalyptic, and in the closely
related scheme of reward and punishment, and in the

limitation of their activity to Israel — a limitation natural enough at that time. The decisive attitude toward this world and the next, with its deep seriousness, with its hope and longing, with its anxiety in view of the final woes and its simple joy over the speedy coming of the end, and likewise the narrowness of its outlook on the world, found here in the circle of these convinced followers of the Messiah its true home.

CHAPTER XI

THE TRANSITION TO UNIVERSALISM, *i.e.* TO HELLENISM

On account of their close connection we may next consider two tendencies in the life of primitive Christianity which though flowing side by side were independent of each other: one, recognizable in the uppermost level of the tradition in the Gospel of Mark, i.e. in the editorial revision of that Gospel; the other, finding its literary expression in the special tradition of Luke, and in all essentials sharing the same outlook as the third evangelist.

The confluence of these two streams of tradition is indicated first in the preference for certain literary types familiar to Hellenism, which may be described as miracle stories, biographical apothegms and legends, and to which may be added the typical illustrative stories found in the Gospel of Luke.[1]

Even more important for us, however, is the relationship of ideas, in which the following points are characteristic:

(a) The relaxation of the eschatological tension as Salvation came to be viewed as a possession in this present life (the antecedents of conversion, bodily and spiritual restoration).

(b) The appearance of the ' enthusiastic ' way of life

and the conception of the Holy Spirit as its inspirer and sustainer.

(c) The resolute breaking down of national limitations (the interest in the heathen and Samaritans).

(d) A wider social outlook — the interest in the despised, in women, publicans, and the morally outcast.

(e) The beginnings of Christian hero-worship in the form of the growth of legend about the figure of Peter, as the leading apostle.

I. The Decline of the Eschatological Hope in View of the Possession of Salvation in the Present

As we turn from the Logia and the oldest sections of the Gospel of Mark, to Mark in its present form and to the Lucan special matter, we observe at once a remarkable contrast, notably in the relaxation of the eschatological tension, i.e. the exclusive concentration of interest upon the end of the age, the coming of the Son of Man, and redemption from this present 'perishing' world. In its place we detect an unmistakable interest in salvation and redemption as already accomplished by Jesus upon earth. This leads, in fact, to the production of the 'gospel' in the literary sense, namely, the account of Jesus' earthly ministry of salvation. Paul had already laid weight upon the redemptive activity which the Christian was able to trace even in the present. However, this activity was, as he viewed it, really a gift of the exalted Lord, i.e. the fruit of the Death and Resurrection of Christ. As far as the earthly life of the Sav-

iour was concerned, apart from the fact of his coming
into the world and his self-humiliation, Paul took no
interest in it. However, sometime during the first generation, and before the destruction of Jerusalem, the
decisive change took place. For several reasons it must
be assumed that this interest was simultaneous with the
rise of the new Gentile-Christian tendency in the primitive church — a view which is all the more reasonable
since the Hellenistic world, with its own distinctive,
non-Jewish outlook, must have found the prevailing
one-sided, eschatological-apocalyptic attitude thoroughly strange and unfamiliar.

We may therefore easily understand the conviction
we meet with in that stage of the Synoptic tradition
which may be called the Hellenistic or universalistic
stratum of tradition and revision, which was probably
to be found even in Jerusalem but was chiefly identified
with Syria, Asia Minor, and Rome — the conviction,
namely, that salvation is not only a possession in the
future, which the Son of Man will confer upon his own
after the world-judgment, but is something that Jesus
has already brought into existence upon earth. In place
of the hitherto accepted but crude division of time into
the old earthly age, now passing away, and the new
heavenly age or aeon, now appeared a three-fold division: the old age, the present era which saw the coming of salvation upon earth, and the completed salvation
in the future; in this scheme the emphasis is placed
upon the second division. This period of the arrival
of salvation, which enables those who participate in it

to enjoy in advance the blessedness of the final consummation, has certain clear signs: Jesus' own work as
Saviour, the conversion of the outcast, the healing of the
sick, and the outpouring of the Holy Spirit. Jesus' saying was fulfilled: ' If I by the power of the Spirit of God
cast out demons, then the Kingdom of God has already
come to you ' (Matt. xii. 28; Luke xi. 20); and also that
other saying: ' The blind see, the lame walk, the lepers
are cleansed, the dead are raised up, and the poor have
the gospel preached to them. . . . Blessed is he who
shall find no occasion of stumbling in me ' (Matt. xi. 4f;
Luke vii. 22f). It was from this point of view that
Mark worked, aiming to meet a real need of the time,
and gathering together the materials for the first of all
the narratives of the wonderful works of Jesus — which
in many respects remind us of the *thaumasta erga*
(marvellous deeds) of the Hellenistic prophets and
teachers of religion, and also of the Epiphany-stories of
Gods and Sons of Gods in the Hellenistic religious
world. The miracle-working Son of Man Messiah received thus the name ' Son of God,' a title which would
be far more readily understood by Gentile Christian
readers (cf. Mark i. 1, 11; xv. 39). Even while he was
upon earth his divine might was manifest, especially
in his power over the spirits of darkness, who had
gained control over suffering humanity. From the
first chapter onward, Mark undertakes to demonstrate
this: the poor victim of mental aberration, the leper, the
lame man, the dumb, the blind, and the epileptic, all
experience in body and soul the saving power of the

Son of God, and even the dead (e.g. the daughter of Jairus) are roused out of their sleep. In the same way men are freed from the bondage of an external fulfilment of the Law and a dead sacrificial worship. But by no means do all recognize their liberator. For the most part it is only the beings in the spiritual world, the demons who dwell in the bodies of the sick; and then —almost the only representative of humanity (after Simon Peter) —the heathen centurion at the cross, since for the spiritually blind people the appearance of the Messiah remained incomprehensible, and even his own disciples were not able to grasp his revelation made in lowly humility.

In addition to the physically ill, it is the spiritually ill and the morally outcast, the sinners and publicans, who share in this salvation. It is not the 'righteous,' but the 'sinners,' to whom the Son of Man has come.

This line of development, already clearly apparent in Mark, becomes a leading motive in the special material and in the editorial revision of the Gospel of Luke: the arrival of the era of salvation manifests itself not only in physical restoration but chiefly in turning from sin. A series of vivid conversion-stories is contained in the special Lucan tradition. To it belong the narratives of the Lost Son, the Lost Coin, the Lost Sheep, the Pharisee and the Publican, the colorful biographic apothegms of the woman that was a sinner, of the Publican Zacchaeus, and of the crucified robber: ' *Today* is salvation come to this house,' 'Thy sins *are* forgiven,' 'Verily, I say unto thee, *today* shalt thou be with me in Paradise' — these are the important sayings about which the narratives are constructed (Luke vii. 48; xix. 9; xxiii. 43). It is through deep agitation of soul that sinful humanity must pass in order to share in redemption. Overcome by shame and sorrow over their past life, criminals, harlots, and servants of Mammon become new men and women through their contact with Jesus. Heaven opens above them, even in this world, and the celestial joy over the restoration of the lost is expressed in the cry of triumph: 'Rejoice with me, for this my son was lost, and is found; he was dead, and is alive again' (Luke xv. 24, 32).

This religion of the present, as we may call it, is characterized by deep human motives and experiences. In addition to contrition and the sense of guilt, which led to forgiveness (see the stories of the Lost Son, the Woman that was a Sinner, the Pharisee and the Publican), there are also examples of earnest spiritual devotion (Mary and Martha), of compassionate humanity rising above national limitations (the Good Samaritan), of the feeling of gratitude (the Samaritan leper who was cleansed), of sympathy with innocent suffering (the women of Jerusalem weeping for Jesus), and others. Real human feeling and good deeds count for more, even in heaven, than the external fulfilment of the Law, the privileges of position or of rank, or the fact that one belongs to the 'righteous' or to the 'chosen' people. One of the weightiest questions for research is the degree in which this human Christianity of the present, which experienced the transcendent Sal-

vation as something immanent, goes back to Jesus himself or to a type of Palestinian Christianity directly
dependent upon him. The representative figures,
Samaritan, Publican, Pharisee — as also the local background, the temple, the city of Jericho, the house of a
friend (in Bethany) — all point to Palestine. On the
other hand, the style of the narratives is Hellenistic.
In the same direction, i.e. toward the Hellenistic sphere,
appear to point also the high value placed upon bodily
healing, and likewise the role played by the phenome-
non of religious abandon or enthusiasm, which is directly assigned to the activity of a special divine power,
the Holy Spirit.

II. The Holy Spirit as the Source of Religious Enthusiasm and His Activities

The Spirit of God, sometimes simply referred to as
the 'Spirit,' is found here and there even in the oldest
stratum of tradition, where it is closely connected with
Old Testament usage ('the Spirit of Yahweh'): e.g.
Jesus will not baptize with water but with the Spirit
and with fire. It is in the power of the Spirit that he
drives out the demons. When the persecuted disciples
are haled before the court it is the Spirit which will
give them utterance. In the few passages in the older
stratum where the Spirit appears, it is not the 'Holy
Spirit' in the specific Christian sense that is referred
to, as the sign of the era of salvation which has now
arrived, or, what is the same thing, of the Christian
dispensation; but rather, just as in the Old Testament,

it is a designation for unique and extraordinary activities far surpassing human ability.

A somewhat different situation is found in the Hellenistic stratum. Even in Mark the view appears that the 'Holy Spirit' is a power specially given to Christians (note the form taken in Mark xiii. 11 by the words of Q, in Matthew x. 20, concerning the Spirit who will supply the disciples with the right reply). In Luke the 'Holy Spirit' becomes the definite sign of the Christian era of salvation, which has now come to pass, and it is used almost as a technical term. This appears most clearly in the Book of Acts, where the pouring forth of the Holy Spirit brings the Christian community into existence, and where every missionary success with its accompanying signs, especially those of a miraculous nature — healings, visions, premonitions, the gift of inspired utterance, the strength to face martyrdom, the speaking with tongues — are all traced back directly to the Holy Spirit as their author (e.g. Acts ii. 4, 16–18; vi. 10; vii. 55; viii. 29; ix. 31; x. 19; xi. 12, 28 and elsewhere). But not only in Acts. Luke has also retouched the picture of Jesus' life and presents it much more clearly than Mark does in the light of the conception of the Holy Spirit. It is through a miraculous activity of the Holy Spirit that the Annunciation becomes effective. Filled with the Holy Spirit, Zacharias and Elizabeth, the aged Simeon and the prophetess Anna hail the approaching day of redemption and greet the young Saviour (Luke i. 41, 67; ii. 27). Armed with the Holy Spirit Jesus overcomes the tempter (iv. 1).

To his disciples he promises the gift of the Holy Spirit,
in the saying on the divine response to prayer (xi. 13;
contrast Matt. vii. 11); and at his departure he an-
nounces to them the outpouring of the Spirit, which is
to be their proper equipment for their calling as missionaries. Prediction, inspired speech, miraculous in-
tuitions, the healing of the sick, the readiness to suffer
martyrdom — these are the chief manifestations in
which the power of the Holy Spirit is evident. All this
forces us to the conclusion that the conception of the
'Holy Spirit' was inseparable from the new stage of
Hellenistic Christianity, with which it grew up, and
which we must suppose to have been a Christianity of
out-and-out religious enthusiasm. It was not at the
beginning of the Jewish-Christian community in Jerusalem, but at the beginning of the Gentile-Christian
movement that the 'outpouring of the Spirit' belonged,
with its characteristic ecstatic-enthusiastic manifestations. *It was primarily the Gentile-Christian community which was the community of the Holy Spirit.*[2]

We may thus contrast explicitly the Jewish-Christian
stage with its Son of Man dogma, and the Hellenistic
with its activities of the Spirit (one recalls in this connection the ideas of St. Paul, who combined the two).
Aware that they were in possession of a power destined
to overcome the world and its peoples, the adherents
of the new movement had the courage to overstep the
limits of the Jewish religion and, confident of the future, to open the way to a purely spiritual worship of
God without temple or sacrifice. The forms of the

Jewish synagogue became too narrow and were unable to hold back the stream of the new religion, which now gave itself to the task of spreading over ' the whole world.'

There is an interesting passage in the Synoptic tradition which illustrates this transition from the Son of Man doctrine to the Christianity of the Spirit. This is the section or *pericope* regarding the ' sin against the Holy Spirit.' While it appears in the older form in Matthew xii. 31 as apparently a blasphemy of the Spirit (without the attribute ' Holy '), a meaning compatible with the Pharisaic suspicion of collusion with Beelzebub, and accordingly identical with aspersions upon Jesus' divine mission, the later additions and revisions (Matt. xii. 32; cf. Mark iii. 29; Luke xii. 10) speak of a sin against the ' Holy Spirit,' compared with which the ' blasphemy against the Son of Man ' appears as something quite different and indeed less serious and more easily forgiven. In this shifting of accent we may clearly perceive the transition from the first phase to the era of the Holy Spirit. Elsewhere in the same stratum of tradition the view that resistance to the Spirit and blasphemy of it is the monstrous act of hardening of the human heart, which thus excludes itself forever from salvation (Acts vii. 51; v. 3, 9). Further evidence of the decisive part taken by possession of the Spirit is found also in the distinction between specifically Christian baptism (the ' Baptism of the Spirit ') and the original baptism of water, in the writings of Luke (Acts viii. 15, 16; x. 44–48; xix. 1ff).

III. THE FINAL BREAKING DOWN OF
NATIONAL LIMITATIONS

A further implication of the new step was the complete abandonment of Jewish particularism. Even at the 'Son of Man' stage, as we have seen, the national and legal limitations of the Jewish religion were already inwardly in a measure overcome. The Son of Man was thought of as the judge of *all* peoples. By his relation to the Son of Man and to his 'brother' was determined the destiny of the individual. The influx of the heathen into the Kingdom of God belonged among the events which were to precede the end. Incidentally, even here is found the saying, 'Verily, I have not found so great faith, no, not in Israel!' (Matt. viii. 10ff; cf. Luke vii. 9, probably from Q). The outward forms of Jewish worship — the temple cultus, sacrifices, cleansings, circumcision, etc. — had lost their significance. At the same time the idea of a position of special privilege for Israel survived: its conversion was absolutely prerequisite to the coming of the end; indeed, the followers of the Messiah, with the college of the twelve apostles at their head, were none other than the true Israel of the end of the age, the nucleus of the People of God.

Soon, however, thanks to the free movement of the Spirit, even these limitations were broken down. The Spirit bloweth where he listeth and is not restrained by any bonds of nationality. Even Mark thinks with pleasure of the incident from the life of Jesus, when he

extended his work to the half-heathen population of
Decapolis and won success there (Mark v. 20; vii. 31).
A Greek Syro-Phoenician woman is praised by Jesus
for her faith and receives her petition (Mark vii. 24ff).
The heathen centurion at the cross becomes, as we saw,
one of the first confessors of Jesus' divine Sonship, while
the Jews, on the other hand, were responsible for his
death (Mark xv. 39). And in the view of the condition
to be met before the final consummation there has
taken place a complete change: it is no longer the
evangelization of Israel, but the preaching of the gospel
among all the nations of the earth (Mark xiii. 10) —
which implies a complete alteration of the older eschatological conception of the coming of the end. This
represents an enormous widening of the horizon compared with the outlook of the primitive Jewish Christian community. We understand perfectly that the
strongly Jewish conception of the apostles seated on
twelve thrones, judging the twelve tribes of Israel, had
no further meaning for the circle about Mark, and in
its stead an entirely different reward is promised to
Peter, as also to the sons of Zebedee, and in their person
to the other apostles as well (Mark x. 28ff, 35ff).

Luke carries out the abandonment of the nationalistic
principle still more consistently. Here it is chiefly the
' Samaritans ' who obviously represent the non-Jewish
world. It is generally recognized to be one of Luke's
favorite ideas, that Jesus gave himself to the despised
Samaritans with the same redeeming love which he
lavished upon his own people. He was not careful to

avoid their territory, as were other Jews (Luke ix. 51ff; xvii. 11). In the parable of the Good Samaritan it is only a Samaritan, and none of the Jewish temple officials, who fulfils the commandment of love for one's neighbor (x. 33ff); and again it is a Samaritan who alone of the ten lepers that were cleansed does not forget to return thanks for his healing, but moved by the feeling of thankfulness returns to Jesus and gives glory to God (xvii. 15ff). We will probably make no mistake if we explain the role assigned to Samaritans in the Gospel of Luke by the fact that the Samaritan mission marked the crest of the wave in the movement toward universalism in primitive Christianity, concerning which the Book of Acts tells us in Chapter viii.

IV. The Widening of the Social Outlook

A no less characteristic enlargement of the common consciousness is to be found in relation to the various social groups and classes. It is true, the primitive Jewish-Christian community was by no means an exclusive class association. However, as a result of the sharp distinction drawn between it and the ' world,' it does not seem to have been entirely free from a certain tendency in the direction of religious provincialism, the conventicle outlook, which easily fails to recognize the great diversity and variety of social life. The uncomplicated social structure of provincial life had its influence even upon the organization of the Christian community. But this situation was destined to be altered. With the collapse of Jewish nationalistic limitations, Christianity found itself set in the midst of a flowing tide of activity in the great cities of Syria and Asia Minor, Greece and Italy. Here there were no longer to be found those who had been called ' the quiet in the land.' In addition to the mass of day laborers, manual workers, soldiers and unemployed, there were men and women who had been beguiled by the deceiving brilliance of city life, officials who had become well-to-do by questionable means, young people driven to and fro between merely sensuous well-being and peace of soul; and in addition, there were the other great contrasts between the rich and the poor, the rulers and the ruled, and likewise the far more complicated problems of family life and of the social position of woman than in the Jewish province. Thus the new religion of universal childhood to God found itself faced with the task of carrying on a complicated social mission, which as far as possible was to include all classes and groups. It was only natural, therefore, that the norms derived from the primitive ' conventicle' stage no longer sufficed. The time had come to outgrow these. This took place through the recognition and further unfolding of a hitherto scarcely noticed principle of the gospel of Jesus, his openness to all the most varied relations of human life.

Even in Mark, much more clearly than in the collection of Sayings, this openness of attitude on Jesus' part is emphasized. One recalls his participation in the publicans' dinner and his free and unprejudiced attitude toward the question of fasting, in Mark ii. 13ff; as also the note of sympathy even for the rich, in Mark x. 21, which was probably designed to soften the rigorous and unyielding attitude of the primitive community with its ' ebionite ' attitude; and also Jesus' recognition of the value of marriage and his love of children, Mark x. 2ff. In Luke we find this recognition of the manifold variety of social groups and their interrelations still more strongly emphasized. Neither the rich and prominent citizen nor the beggar in his utter misery, neither the well-to-do land-owner nor the newly rich official, whose success in life has been achieved by unscrupulous methods, the disreputable woman, the adventurer wandering in the by-ways, nor the condemned murderer and robber is lacking in Luke's rich gallery of portraits. Various economic and social relationships receive here a Christian illumination. The various ages of man find here their representatives. Chiefly, however, it is the human condition and the specific spiritual disposition of woman, which is a subject of extraordinary interest in this Gospel. This interest is witnessed by the various women who appear in its pages: the aged Elizabeth, Anna with her gift of prophecy, the women who accompanied Jesus and ministered unto him of their substance, Mary Magdalene from whom ' seven demons ' had been driven out, the woman in the crowd who pronounced Jesus' Mother blessed, the great sinner of Luke vii, the devout and contemplative Mary and her active and energetic sister Martha, the widow untiring in her petition, the women of Jerusalem with their deep human sympathy, and above all others the Virgin Mother of Jesus, who is pronounced 'blessed among women' and yet is at the same time the *Mater Dolorosa*.

We must acknowledge that a development has taken place in the knowledge of the human soul in its manifold individual variations, as affected by social condition, sex, position and age, a feature which harmoniously supplements the world-wide universalism and the specifically Christian concern for the fallen. One may observe this in the second concluding formula of the Parable of the Great Supper in Luke; after the crippled, the blind and the lame have already been brought in, the servant is commanded, 'Go out into highways and hedges, and compel them to come in, that my house may be *filled!*' (Luke xiv. 23).

V. The Beginnings of the Petrine Legend

This change from the conventicle outlook and the provincial conditions of the primitive community to the world-embracing attitude of Hellenistic Christianity could not take place except in firm contact with the early tradition and through express appeal to a generally recognized authority of the first generation of disciples. This authority was Peter, whose rise to the position of unquestioned leadership in the Church and to that of the ideal disciple of Christ was contemporaneous with the emergence of the universalistic Christianity of the Spirit. It is an extremely interesting question, but one hitherto insufficiently explained, how it came to pass that this tendency in early Christianity, open as it was to the world, universalistic and enthusiastic and concerned with the common man, was inspired by the person of Peter. Apparently the first suggestion came from the fact that Peter was really the most important of the companions of Jesus. Moreover, he was the leading witness upon whom the faith in the Resurrection rested, and the one about whom the scattered disciples first rallied. Still other factors were involved: neither James, on account of his narrow attitude toward the Gentiles, nor Paul, since he lacked the qualification of a witness of the earthly life of Jesus, was eligible to serve as leader of the general Christian movement in the same way as Peter. Of great significance for the feeling of the time, which laid much emphasis upon ecstatic experiences, is the appearance of the apostle in the role of visionary, and his receiving of 'revelations.' Thus he became the 'witness,' without whose authority the 'dynastic' and traditionalist tendency of the Jerusalem community, which found its champion in James, could never have been overcome or the unity of the Church been maintained intact.

His position of leadership, which at the level of the Palestinian Logia-tradition (Q) is by no means clearly recognizable, begins to be apparent in Mark. In the composition of the Gospel of Mark the specific Petrine sections are clearly distinguishable, beginning with his call beside the sea of Gennesaret and Jesus' visit at Peter's house in Capernaum, and then, in further succession, Peter with John and James at the house of Jairus, Peter's Confession, Peter with the other two disciples as witnesses of the Transfiguration, Peter at the Last Supper, in the Garden of Gethsemane, and in the court of the high priests' palace, Peter named in the message of the angel to the women (Mark xvi. 7). In Luke we find passages in which the person of Peter is much more clearly portrayed in his later role of leadership, and engaged in the task of the Gentile Mission, especially in the section relating Peter's draught of fishes (Luke v) and his commission as fisher of men; the pointing in Peter's direction of the saying regarding the faithful steward (Luke xii. 41ff); the command addressed to Peter in the hour of trial to 'strengthen his brethren' (xxii. 31f), and the notice given the appearance of the Risen Lord to Peter (xxiv. 34); as also the description of the scene in Gethsemane, in which the apostle appears in a somewhat more favorable light; and finally the Petrine narratives of the Book of Acts, which characteristically portray him in the role of leader.

It has often been thought that the Petrine sections in the Gospel of Mark go back to the personal reminiscences of the disciple who, as the statement of Papias has been interpreted to mean, provided the substance of the tradition of which Mark made use as his 'translator' or interpreter. This hypothesis may contain a kernel of truth. However, one must not overlook the fact that in certain passages, e.g. x. 28ff and likewise viii. 29 and xvi. 7, Peter is already idealized as the head and leader of the disciples. This is still more apparent in Luke (we are disregarding Matthew for the time being), where Peter is charged with the world-mission

(Luke v), and in fact, proceeds to fulfil it (Acts ii, iii,
iv, x, xi). His weaknesses fade gradually into forgetfulness (note the softening of these features in the accounts of Gethsemane and the Denials, as also the
suppression of Peter's all-too-human protest at the announcement of Jesus' sufferings (Luke ix. 21ff); instead, he appears more and more as the faithful steward,
the foundation pillar of the Resurrection faith, the com-
forter and strengthener of the other brethren, and the
recipient of special revelations. This line of development finds notable continuation in the Gospel of
Matthew.

What is the conclusion we are to draw from these
facts? It seems to me, the following: The period of the
earliest witnesses of the life of Jesus came more and
more to be viewed as the heroic age of the beginnings
of Christianity, the period of the first great conflicts, vic-
tories and marvels. The need for heroic leading figures
stood closely connected with the lessening of the eschatological tension and the glorification of the might of the
Spirit and the entry of Christianity into the Hellenistic
sphere of culture, with its tendency to hero-worship.
This need was soon met by the heroizing of the person
of Peter as the supreme leader of the church. Referred
back to him, the great transition in primitive Christianity received its full and now no longer to be contested
justification.

Finally, it is an interesting and important question
where this decisive transition to universalism began.
It would surely be no mistake to say that it must have

received strongest support in the great Hellenistic cities, such as Antioch, Tarsus and Ephesus. In the earliest period Antioch was without doubt of decisive importance. However, in view of the tradition, the conclusion must be drawn that the beginnings even of this movement are to be sought within the borders of Palestine. The roots of the Gospel of Mark go back clearly to Jerusalem and Galilee, as both its topography and its description of the background show. Moreover, the special tradition in the Gospel of Luke — one thinks of the Parable of the Good Samaritan, the story of Zacchaeus the Publican, the Parable of the Pharisee and the Publican, and above all the Nativity and Infancy narratives — this tradition still has, with few exceptions, a Palestinian coloring. One must therefore agree with those scholars who find the origin of this tendency even in the primitive community, perhaps in the circle of Stephen and Philip; which is as much as to say that the tendency was already at work in Jerusalem, and then, its leaders driven from the metropolis by Jewish persecution, it spread through Samaria, Galilee and Syria, where it made itself most at home.[3]

CHAPTER XII

THE TRANSITION TO ECCLESIASTICISM AND CHRISTIAN RABBINISM (THE MATTHAEAN TRADITION)

The Gospel of Matthew has a strongly expressed and distinct individuality. It possesses a much greater understanding of Judaism than Mark and Luke, and indeed, to some extent, even than the Logia (Q). On the other hand, it draws the line between the old and the new theocracy, Judaism and universal Christianity, no less sharply than do Paul, Mark, and Luke. The Vineyard of the Lord, the Kingdom of Heaven, or however else it may be designated, now belongs, because of the monstrous obduracy of the Jews, to a people who bring forth fruit in its season (Matt. xxi. 41 and 43 — much more strongly emphasized than in Luke and Mark), i.e. those who stood outside and were not among those originally called (xxii. 7ff). It is the detailed exposition of the idea of the New Theocracy, which had its heralds and forerunners in the prophets but first made its appearance through the Son of God, and was thus both parallel to and contrasted with the Mosaic stage of revelation.

One may question whether or not this is the work of an individual who placed upon the traditional material the stamp of his own personality, rather than that a

THE TRANSITION TO ECCLESIASTICISM

view which dominated some new collective spiritual development of the common Christian life has here received expression. Nowhere else in the Synoptic Gospels has the formulation and arrangement of material been determined with such rigid consistency as here. On the other hand, the following considerations deserve to be noted. The Gospel of Matthew makes use of extremely distinctive sections of *community* tradition, in which the peculiarities are most clearly recognizable: e.g. vi. 1–18; xiii. 36–52; xvi. 16–19; xvii. 24–27; xviii. 15–35, passages in which much more clearly than in the peculiar matter of Luke the existence of an organized community is presupposed. In this and in similar material, as also in the arrangement of the Gospel as a whole which bears the same peculiar mark, we may observe an undeniable tendency (a) from the originally loosely organized common life of a brotherhood of Christian believers to the developed theocratic ecclesiasticism under the ' primacy of Peter,' with Word and sacrament, a sense of missionary obligation, and a rigid discipline; and (b) from the Spirit-filled life to a teaching or doctrine resting upon scribism.

I. The Idea of the Church

For Matthew far more than for Mark the return of the Son of Man is removed to a distance. Jerusalem has already been destroyed (xxii. 7), and yet ' the bridegroom ' continues to delay (xxv. 5 and 19). In this connection there is a new attitude taken toward the idea of the Kingdom of Heaven. In a sense it has al-

ready begun here upon earth. The period of waiting,
originally looked upon as destined to be brief, has now
become more or less the normal situation. This may
be noted especially in the specifically Matthaean parables of the Kingdom of Heaven and their explanation
(Matt. xiii). The Kingdom of Heaven is like a field
in which the seed grows under various conditions. It is
like a field where many tares grow amid the stalks of
wheat. It is like a drag net in which not only good but
also bad fish have been caught. It is quite clear that the
Kingdom of Heaven (in its earthly stage) is nothing
more nor less than a new kind of fellowship, the
Church. The tares in the field, which may originally
have stood for the evil in the world, are now made to
mean, in the interpretation offered in this Gospel, the
wicked men whose father is the devil and who are, unfortunately, to be found even within the Church. This
reflects a great decline in the purity of the common life.
However, there is this much consolation: things will
not always be this way. At the 'end of the world' the
evil will be separated from the good and given up to
destruction, whereas the righteous will shine like the
sun in their Father's Kingdom (xiii. 40ff, 49f; cf. xxv.
31–46).

The extension of the period of waiting into the state
of normal continuance undoubtedly took place in the
consciousness of the community; cf. xxviii. 20, 'Lo, I
am with you alway, even unto the end of the world.'
Meanwhile, the true characteristic of this present
earthly stage of the Kingdom of Heaven is not the en-

thusiastic response to the guidance of the Spirit, as in Luke, but the realization of the theocracy in the form of the Church. The word *ecclesia* occurs in the Gospels but twice, and then only in Matthew. It occurs in the classical passage Matthew xvi. 17–18, where it clearly bears the meaning of the collective Church as an exclusive institution; and also in Matthew xviii. 17, where the reference is to the organized local church. If for no other reasons, these facts alone suffice to show that the apologetic attempt to find the church-idea in the oldest evangelic material (as most recently by K. L. Schmidt in the *Festgabe* for Deissmann) must be abandoned. It is not until we reach the period of the Matthaean tradition that we come upon the attempt to trace back the founding of the Church to Jesus.

The same applies to church organization and discipline, to which the passage, Matthew xviii, is devoted. Matthew applies the word for 'little ones' (*mikroi*) to the members of the church, and likewise applies the devastating ' woes ' to those who cause them to stumble. The sad fact that there were already those who had been led astray is thus indirectly indicated. The question had arisen: What was to be done with those who had fallen under such destructive influences and were beginning to deny their faith? How were they to be restored? The answer is found in the passage already referred to, xviii. 15–20. Corresponding to the Jewish practice, three stages of procedure are recommended: a private admonition, then an admonition in the presence of one or two witnesses, finally, a public rebuke in the presence of the assembled congregation. With this, however, the limits of gentleness and clemency have been reached: all other means unavailing, nothing remained but expulsion from the fellowship, or, as was said, 'Let the guilty be to you as a heathen or a publican.' Contrasted with the generous-hearted Lucan attitude, this seems very rigorous, and can scarcely be viewed as anything but a revival of the Jewish practice of excommunication within the new Christian movement. As if the author himself realized the danger that lay in such a process of 'judgment,' he adds, at the end of the chapter, the Parable of the Unforgiving Debtor — a moving exhortation to unconditional readiness to forgive personal injury (xviii. 23-35).

To the administration of congregational discipline and the imposition of penance belonged the exercise of an authority which possessed the *potestas clavium* or 'power of the keys,' i.e. the right to impose excommunication in the name of Jesus. In the passage already referred to, xviii. 18, 19, it is still the assembled congregation itself (or, perhaps, the college of the Twelve?) through whom the Spirit speaks and in whose midst the exalted Lord himself responds to the prayer of the disciples, and makes the decision. This is at any rate the earlier situation, and corresponds to a time when no one had as yet thought of a monarchical administration of the community.

However, as time went by the course of development took other directions. Whether in consequence of the developing Jewish synagogue organization in the period following the destruction of Jerusalem,[1] or under the influence of other factors — it is hard to say which — there arose at any rate, about the end of the first century, in Syria and Palestine, a tendency to place at the head of the community a single authoritative person whose powers could be traced back to Christ himself. In this connection it was possible for the idea to arise that Christ himself had committed to one of his disciples the disciplinary (and perhaps the teaching) authority of his *ecclesia*. Corresponding to the significant surname of Simon, *Kephas* (i.e. Rock), which usage undoubtedly goes back to Jesus himself, Simon was designated as the Rock upon which the Lord meant to found his church. Through the use of primitive symbolism he was honored as the possessor of the keys of the Kingdom of Heaven, and the authority was ascribed to him to ' bind ' and to ' loose,' i.e. not merely to pronounce forbidden or permitted (cf. Strack-Billerbeck on Matt. xvi. 17f), but to retain sins and to absolve — in other words to pronounce or to dissolve the ban upon sinners. Thus the *ecclesia* received in him its hierarchical head, its first divinely commissioned leader and ' Prince of the Church,' whom apparently the Syrian Church was the first to honor, and thus gave fixed form to the idea of the monarchical episcopate.

What had now come to pass? The figure of Peter, the model of the disciple restored by grace after his fall, the great missionary, who casts the net of the Kingdom of Heaven for its catch, is on the way to become the foundation of the developing church, and thus to occupy a position of dignity similar to that of Christ, equipped with full authority, not only to safeguard the purity of the community, but also to share in determining the eternal destiny of its members. In the same context belong the other Petrine sections in the Matthaean tradition, e.g. xiv. 28ff, where he is the only one of the disciples who at the behest of the Master walks upon the tempestuous waves of the sea, and xvii. 24-27, where in the person of Peter the (Jewish-Christian) community receives the direction to contribute, for the sake of peace, the required temple tax, even though their members were, as children of the Kingdom, free from this obligation — a passage which shows how close and strong were the bonds which still held it to the synagogue![2]   Finally, we must refer again to the Petrine section in Matthew xviii. 21ff.   One may easily recognize the motive for the incipient preference of the Church for the Gospel of Matthew: it is its concern with the organization and inner life of the community, both alike decked with the authority of Jesus and also that of the Rock-disciple, and its appreciation of rigid organization and control.   Every group in the developing church that longed for an ecclesiastical 'legislation' and a centralized control, in order to achieve inner unity and strength to resist the hostile aggression of the Jewish Synagogue, rallied about this Gospel. Here, and here only, was it clearly stated that Jesus himself had been concerned to secure a stable organization of the Church's life, had not only set forth the fundamental principles of the new ethics but also given rules to apply to the questions of fasting, prayer, and alms-giving, instituted not only the Lord's Supper but also the sacrament of Baptism, gave strict command for the Gentile Mission, and thus himself laid the foundation of the Church with its Word and sacraments. Where, however, further directions and ordinances were lack-ing, he had given to the leaders of the community, in the person of Peter, the authority to provide them.

II. Doctrine

What has just been said leads us a step further, since it shows us how, contemporaneously with the centering of the interest of the community in the idea of the Church, there arose the need for a definitely formulated teaching or doctrine, which came as the product of Christian scribism. In the developed doctrinal teaching of the Gospel of Matthew we can distinguish a number of different elements.

First of all, there is the teaching concerning the ' new righteousness ' or morality. This is contained in Chap-ter v, which begins the Sermon on the Mount — in the so-called antitheses. In general this section reflects ac-curately the principles of the eschatologically-minded, world-renouncing early Christians. Now as before, it is reconciliation, absolute honesty, purity in the relations of the sexes, the victory over evil achieved through love, which are central for ethics. At the same time the de-velopment has already led to a certain externalization and casuistic weakening of the great absolute impera-tive. The ' new righteousness ' is no longer set over

against the Pharisaic ethics, in an absolute contrast, but
is preferred as outbidding the latter in the measure of
its earnest fulfilment of the Law (v. 19, 20); thus the
'legal' point of view is introduced into the ethics of
the community. In the warning against the sin of
anger (v. 21f), a casuistic scheme has been introduced.
The principle of the absolute indissolubility of marriage
and the equality of woman loses, through the addition
of a clause, its original sublimity and impressiveness (v.
32). Even the substitution, in place of an oath, of the
solemn formula of asseveration, the doubled 'Yea' or
'Nay' (v. 37), scarcely corresponds to the original
meaning of the saying (cf. James v. 12). On the other
hand, the command to love one's enemy appears in its
wholly primitive and unaffected sublimity, though even
this has received additions which reflect the Christian
awareness of a sharp distinction between themselves
and their neighbors and their expectation of a higher
reward than that awaiting the heathen and publicans
(v. 46f).

A further element in the doctrinal teaching is the
section dealing with the new forms of piety (vi. 1–18).
Corresponding to the traditional Semitic triad — alms,
prayer, fasting — the general point of view is the common Christian one of absolute inwardness. Even here,
however, the system of rewards begins to make its appearance. A certain externalism is to be noted even in
the words introducing the Lord's Prayer: 'After this
manner therefore pray ye' (vi. 9) — words that really
contradict those found in the preceding verse and show

that emphasis was already being laid upon the sacredness of the formula itself, though not yet in the absolute legalistic sense which we come upon later in the Didache (Did. viii. 2). Similarly, the command regarding fasting in Matthew vi. 16–18 is some stages removed from the primitive rejection of external ordinances.

With this new teaching of ethics and piety corresponds further the conception of Jesus as the new Lawgiver and Fulfiller of the Law, or, we may even say, the Founder of the new religion. This is worked out in a clear parallelism between Jesus and Moses, the founder of the Old Testament religion. Just as the legislation of Moses, so also is that of Jesus delivered upon a mount (v. 1ff). Just as Moses accredited his divine mission by miracles, so likewise did Jesus. Just as Moses chose and sent out twelve heralds, so Jesus sent out his twelve disciples. It was not as one who unsettled the Law but as one who deepened and fulfilled the Law that Jesus appeared. This may be seen in his knowledge of the Law and of scripture, in which he is far superior to the Jewish teachers of the Bible (Matt. xxii). Had anyone before him ever proved so conclusively from the scripture that the Messiah was both Son of God and Son of David (xxii. 41ff)? Or like him set forth the quintessence of the Law in a few words (xxii. 34ff)? It was all to no effect that the Pharisaic scribes and the Sadducees undertook to silence him — through his superior knowledge of the scripture and keenness of utterance he rather silenced them (xxii. 34, 46).

Likewise, as a teacher of wisdom, he showed his su-

periority to all others. This is demonstrated with in-
disputable clarity in the seven parables of the Kingdom
of Heaven (Matt. xiii). An ideal Scribe, he, and the
disciples who followed in his footsteps, knew not only
how to proclaim what was new, but also how to set the
old in a new light and make it useful (xiii. 51f).

However, Jesus is not only the Law-giver and teacher
of wisdom, but also the Messianic King, the Son of
David and Son of God, in whom all the Old Testament
promises and predictions received their fulfilment. In
the twenty passages on the life and work of Jesus in
which the evangelist sees an explicit fulfilment of Old
Testament prediction, this has been clearly pointed out
— note the use of the stereotyped formula, 'that it
might be fulfilled,' and similar expressions. There is
scarcely a significant passage in the history of Jesus
which does not correspond to some Old Testament prediction. His birth of a Virgin and his Davidic ancestry,
Bethlehem as the place of his birth, the coming of the
heathen Wise Men and the presentation of their gifts,
Herod's slaughter of the Innocents and the flight into
Egypt, the appearance of the Baptist, and the activity
of Jesus in a semi-heathen territory, the relieving of the
ill from their diseases, the disclosure of the secrets of
the Kingdom of Heaven, the Messianic entry into Jerusalem, the cleansing of the temple, the children singing
praises, and a whole series of details in the Passion Narrative — all of these have been provided with Old Testament quotations. Thus the whole history of Jesus, by
aid of a Christian scribism, is inwrought with an apolo-

getic body of teaching, further enlarged and buttressed, with the clear purpose of meeting with their own weapons and upon their own territory the strongest opponents of Christianity, the Jewish teachers of the Law. How strong the apologetic tendency became in the development of the tradition is best seen in the reaction to the calumnies and attacks which were launched by the synagogue about this time against certain important Christian teachings. The answer to the charge of Jesus' lowly origin is found in the proof of his descent from Abraham and David (cf. the Genealogy in Matt. i. 1–16); the aspersions cast upon his birth are answered by the story of the angel's message to Joseph, informing him of the miraculous conception (Matt. i. 18–25); the lying reports of the theft of Jesus' body are answered by the account of the sealing of the tomb and the setting of a watch (xxvii. 62ff), as also the bribing of the watch by the Jewish authorities (xxviii. 11–15). It is thus perfectly clear that a series of Christological or, rather, Messianological doctrines, including chiefly those of the Virgin Birth, the descent from David and the disguised Kingship, and the bodily resurrection, were already in process of becoming the inalienable possession of the Great Church.

More or less the same change has taken place with regard to the conception of the last things as took place in regard to moral teaching and Christology. Here also, in place of the unreflective faith and the burning hope of the first witnesses, a somewhat learned view appears, and one that likewise shows the influence of the rabbinic spirit. The view which has already appeared in Mark is now taken for granted, viz. that the end cannot come until the gospel message has been carried to all peoples (xxiv. 14; xxviii. 19); since the world judgment is a judgment of all the nations of the earth (xxiv. 31; xxv. 32), the opportunity must first be given them to declare themselves either for or against Christ. For those who have accepted him and have actually confessed him, paradise awaits; for those who have rejected him, eternal damnation (xxv. 46). This idea of a two-fold destiny in the world to come has grown into one of the most important of ecclesiastical doctrines, while the conception of the endless penalties of hell, which at first were more or less incidental, picturesque, prophetic details, is now granted its full title to a place in dogmatics.

These are only a few examples to show how remote the Matthaean special tradition is from the free and unreflective, non-legal Christianity of the Spirit and of prayer which was to be found in the first decades. It must indeed be admitted that it had come to terms with the widespread universalistic view which was maintained by the victorious Hellenistic tendency, e.g. the prospect of the evangelizing of all nations, the absolute futility of Jewish nationalism, the absurdity of external lustrations, the Sabbath ordinances, and other traits; moreover, the account of the Virgin Birth shows close contact with Hellenism, or rather with Syncretism. In line with this is its sharp criticism of orthodox Palestinian Judaism. And yet, for all this, nowhere in the

Synoptic tradition has the true Jewish spirit more obviously effected an entrance into Christianity than it has here — with its characteristic high regard for scribism and knowledge of the Law, its keen distinction between ' little ' and ' great,' its juristic formulation of the doctrine of reward and punishment, its separation between the chosen of God and the ' Gentiles and publicans.'

CHAPTER XIII

CONCLUSIONS: JESUS AND THE PRIMITIVE CHRISTIAN RELIGION

We have endeavored to sketch briefly the various manifestations of the Christian spirit at its earliest stage, as it must appear to the eyes of the student of the Synoptic Gospels.

It can only be viewed as a serious handicap that we are unable to coordinate completely the various expressions of faith and life within the framework of the external course of events. We must, however, make the best of the scanty knowledge we possess, and make full use of it in our common research today.

It may further be made a matter of complaint that we have not supplemented our three stages of development with a fourth, which should round out the picture of primitive Christian development, and study the Johannine tradition as a new and special manifestation of early Christianity. This tradition had much in common with the other types: with the Palestinian, i.e. the attitude taken toward the other world; with the Hellenistic, i.e. its universalism; with the Matthaean tradition, i.e. the conception of Christ as the founder of the Church (in John a completely spiritualized institution). At the same time, however, the Johannine tradition represented a completely new development, with its introduction of ideas derived from Gnosticism and its mystic inwardness. To pursue such a subject requires special research, of the kind already under way, in order to get beyond mere vague conjectures.

However, even without going into the Johannine tradition-complex, it is quite clear that an interpretation of the gospel tradition in terms of the history of the Christian community has much to offer in the way of a better and richer understanding of the beginnings of Christianity.

It is quite evident that Paul and the author of the Book of Acts were by no means in a position to supply an exhaustive and absolutely impartial account of the life of the early church. Its manifold variety in form is far greater, and its history is far more involved, than the Book of Acts would lead us to suspect. The effort to set forth the content of the new divine revelation in the forms of common human life and thought led very early to a multiplicity of views. In immediate proximity to the childishly credulous eschatological expectation of the Son of Man broke forth a tempestuous religion of the Spirit; side by side with the world-renouncing detachment from earthly things appeared a faith in the world-transforming power of pity and love. And in the midst of a world-accepting spiritual tendency arise unmistakable movements in the direction of a more concretely organized church, with its religious officers, its legal statutes, and an orthodox system of doctrine. Every one of these forms claimed

the same right of appeal to the authentic Gospel of
Jesus, to his directions and his prophetic teaching,
whether it was the expectation of the Parousia within
a brief space of time or the world-wide perspective of
the Gentile Mission, the imposition of the ecclesiastical
ban or an unconditioned readiness to forgive and be
reconciled with one's brother.

The question naturally arises, therefore, Which of
these main expressions best reproduces the spirit of
Jesus, represents him least inadequately, and most con-
sistently unfolds the principles implicit in his Gospel?
(As we have seen, the rigorous legalistic tendency of
James has left scarcely a vestige in the gospel tradition.)

In the answer to this question, which inescapably
presents itself to every student of early Christianity, it
often happens that one or another of these particular
manifestations of primitive Christianity is identified
with the original gospel of Jesus. So, for example,
Albert Schweitzer has done in taking the radical eschatological attitude and Messianic dogma of the oldest
Palestinian group without qualification for the message
of the Founder. The same thing has been done by
many a conservative theologian, especially among
Roman Catholics, with the ecclesiastical tradition in the
Gospel of Matthew. It is only too readily understandable how specialists will succumb to the temptation to
discover in a concrete written stratum of the gospel
text an adequate expression of Jesus' teaching. Here
also we should apply the saying: The Kingdom of God
cometh not ' with outward observation,' so that no one

can say, 'Lo, here, or Lo, there it is.' Though it is un-doubtedly true, as we have seen, that all the secondary developments of tradition were inspired by the Founder and — in varying degrees — find their support in him, not one of them adequately represents him. The deep-est and most essential quality of his gospel was felt to be something transcendent, lying beyond our grasp, something that could only be experienced and could not be set forth didactically; hence there was laid upon his followers the task, in every new array of cir-cumstances to set forth afresh the meaning of their experience and their faith, in a new way of life, in new forms of faith, and in new expressions of religion.

Even this brief survey has demonstrated that already in the course of the first two generations a number of clearly distinguishable types of religious view had emerged, and were already at work shaping the tradition.

The first typical attempt to set forth the nature of the new religion in the form of contemporary thought comes before us in that outlook upon life which we call 'consistent eschatology.' For this type of religious out-look the final Consummation, the coming of God to men, consists in the cessation of things temporal, the 'Parousia' of the Son of Man which is to take place at the end of the age. Consistent with this is the demand, which springs out of a colossal spiritual strain, for a radical separation from 'the world,' from home, posses-sions, and native land, yes, even from wife and child. It is not to be doubted that this outlook as a whole was derived in fact from the message of Jesus, but that, as time went on, as we may see from many examples, there took place an ever more complete shifting of accent and an apocalyptic narrowing down of the original meaning, not infrequently with the result that a completely childish and naive misunderstanding took place, and that an earthly and corporeal outlook became dominant.

The second type looked upon the approaching ' Salvation' as having already arrived in the present; the gates of heaven swung open of their own accord, especially where erring human hearts were broken in penitence and received by grace a new term of life, where the sick became sound, the poor rich, and the dead were brought back to life; where, in brief, these acts of restoration took place here and now within the boundaries of daily life and the present course of nature. Here the victorious universalism of salvation vindicated itself through the obliteration of all human limitations, such as those of a legalistic religion, the feeling of self-righteousness, narrow prejudice and the limitations of language, sex and the like, as among all the peoples of the earth. In this great experience in which the Holy One showed the favors of His grace to sinners, this particular religious type more faithfully interpreted and reproduced the essential nature of the primitive gospel, though many a touch in the gospel, where Christ and sinners are brought in contact, may have been leveled down to mere fine feeling.

In the third type, as a result of the weakening of the

original power of the gospel, the final product has become inadequate to contain or mediate the eternal. Even the few faithful, who once called themselves 'saints,' are interspersed with tares and corruption. The Kingdom of Heaven no longer comes directly to men, but indirectly, through the mediation of sacred institutions. The Church planned and established by Christ, with its doctrine and its law, its sacred ordinances and the office of the keys, is the form through which divine salvation is mediated. Official authority, sacraments, doctrine and law are beginning to be the legitimate channels of the Spirit, no longer flowing freely, but bound now to these institutions. 'Eternal life' is here but the reward of obedience. Nevertheless even in this institutional disguise the divine earnestness of the early days survived, and confronted men with the decision upon which their destiny absolutely depended.

We may accordingly say that at every step in the development there is a real understanding of the original gospel, rooted in genuine experience, and at the same time a certain amount of imaginative and reflective misapprehension of it, though not, however, always in the same proportion.

The original and essential saving gospel displayed itself gradually step by step, and at each separate stage expressed itself in a new manifestation. All the various literary forms, wisdom-saying and prophetic word, controversy, apothegm, miracle-story, cult-legend, and likewise all the varied expressions of life and faith within the community, are but imperfect attempts to conceive the essential nature of the divine revelation and to set it forth and make it effective in the world of appearances. It is, as a whole, to be judged as a kind of childlike stammering about the Absolute, as a speaking in tongues, which may indeed often seem to us mere confusion, on account of its multiplicity of meaning, and alien, since it echoes the tones of a world long past from which it speaks to us. All the same, however, the way that leads us back through this manifold variety and imperfection of utterance and strangeness of appearance leads us in the end to the Founder. The attempt to set forth a scientific conception of Jesus must, therefore, be preceded by a careful and sympathetic study of the faith and the social forms of the community, as they appear to us in the gospel tradition, since it is only from these that his nature and his work can be known, and then only in outline. In the end one comes inevitably to the conclusion that it is chiefly there, where the individual finds himself face to face with an inescapable decision, where the greatest tension is felt between God and man, between the Holy One and the sinner, and where at the same time this gulf between God and man is most completely and most inwardly bridged, since the holy love of God without any mediation of human doctrines or institutions bows in favor to the lowly, that the true nature of the Founder appears before us most clearly and most powerfully.

NOTES

CHAPTER X

[1] Albert Schweitzer looks upon the directions contained in Matthew x. 5 and 23 as typical expressions of Jesus' own eschatological view. On the contrary, unless x. 5 is due to Matthew's editorial revision, we can view them only as reflecting the view of the primitive community or of some group within it and that at the very earliest time.

[2] See also Streeter, *The Four Gospels*, 1926, esp. chh. vii, ix and xvii.

[3] This seems clearly implied in the ancient Eucharistic prayer found in the Didache, chh. ix and x. Cf. J. Weiss, *Das Urchristentum*, 1917; Lietzmann, *Messe und Herrenmahl*, 1926.

CHAPTER XI

[1] Compare on this point Bultmann's *Geschichte der synoptischen Tradition;* ch. viii. pp. 223ff. etc.

[2] Cf. H. Leisegang, *Pneuma Hagion*, where, however, no distinction is drawn between the Old Testament and the Hellenistic conceptions of the Spirit.

[3] Cf. the essay by G. P. Wetter: 'The Oldest Hellenistic Christianity According to the Book of Acts' ('Das älteste hellenistische Christentum nach der Apostelgeschichte,' *Archiv für Rel.-Wiss.*, xxi, 1922).

CHAPTER XII

[1] This was the time when Palestinian Judaism, in the interest of complete cohesion, concentrated for a while the offices of the teacher and the judge in a single person, the Nâsî (i.e. Prince, or Patriarch); cf. Schlatter, *Geschichte des Jüdischen Volkes*, on the person of Gamaliel II.

[2] It is very difficult at the present time to decide whether this pericope is to be dated in the period before the year 70, while the Jewish temple in Jerusalem was still standing, or in the later period when the Roman occupation demanded of the Jews the didrachma for the temple of Jupiter Capitolinus. [It is difficult to suppose that either Christians or Jews would be permitted by their religious authorities to contribute to the latter. Note also that the Jewish legal tradition continued to view the temple as either still standing or sometime to be rebuilt. The Law was binding even when the temple lay in ruins — whether 500 B.C. or 100 A.D.]

HARPER TORCHBOOKS / The University Library

J. Bronowski & Bruce Mazlish	THE WESTERN INTELLECTUAL TRADITION: *From Leonardo to Hegel* TB/3001
Edward P. Cheyney	THE DAWN OF A NEW ERA: 1250–1453. *50 illus.* TB/3002
Carl J. Friedrich	THE AGE OF THE BAROQUE: 1610–1660. *40 illus.* TB/3004
Myron P. Gilmore	THE WORLD OF HUMANISM: 1453–1517. *64 illus.* TB/3003
L. H. Gipson	THE COMING OF THE [AMERICAN] REVOLUTION: 1763–1775. *30 illus.* TB/3007
Wallace Notestein	THE ENGLISH PEOPLE ON THE EVE OF COLONIZATION: 1603–1630. *23 illus.* TB/3006
Louis B. Wright	THE CULTURAL LIFE OF THE AMERICAN COLONIES: 1607–1763. *30 illus.* TB/3005

HARPER TORCHBOOKS / The Academy Library

James Baird	ISHMAEL: *The Art of Melville in the Contexts of Primitivism* TB/1023
Herschel Baker	THE IMAGE OF MAN: *A Study of the Idea of Human Dignity in Classical Antiquity, the Middle Ages, and the Renaissance* TB/1047
Jacques Barzun	THE HOUSE OF INTELLECT TB/1051
W. J. Bate	FROM CLASSIC TO ROMANTIC: *Premises of Taste, 18th Century England* TB/1036
Max Beloff	THE AGE OF ABSOLUTISM, 1660–1815 TB/1062
Jeremy Bentham	THE HANDBOOK OF POLITICAL FALLACIES. Intro. by Crane Brinton TB/1069
Henri Bergson	TIME AND FREE WILL: *The Immediate Data of Consciousness* TB/1021
H. J. Blackham	SIX EXISTENTIALIST THINKERS: *Kierkegaard, Jaspers, Nietzsche, Marcel, Heidegger, Sartre* TB/1002
Crane Brinton	ENGLISH POLITICAL THOUGHT IN THE NINETEENTH CENTURY TB/1071
Walter Bromberg	THE MIND OF MAN: *A History of Psychotherapy and Psychoanalysis* TB/1003
Abraham Cahan	THE RISE OF DAVID LEVINSKY. A novel. Intro. by John Higham TB/1028
Helen Cam	ENGLAND BEFORE ELIZABETH TB/1026
Joseph Charles	THE ORIGINS OF THE AMERICAN PARTY SYSTEM TB/1049
Cochran & Miller	THE AGE OF ENTERPRISE: *A Social History of Industrial America* TB/1054
Norman Cohn	PURSUIT OF THE MILLENNIUM: *Revolutionary Messianism; Medieval and Reformation Europe, its Bearing on Modern Totalitarian Movements* TB/1037
G. G. Coulton	MEDIEVAL VILLAGE, MANOR, AND MONASTERY TB/1022
Wilfrid Desan	THE TRAGIC FINALE: *The Philosophy of Jean-Paul Sartre* TB/1030
Wilhelm Dilthey	PATTERN AND MEANING IN HISTORY: *Thoughts on History and Society.* Edited with Introduction by H. P. Rickman TB/1075
Cora Du Bois	THE PEOPLE OF ALOR: *A Social-Psychological Study of an East Indian Island.* Vol. I, illustrated, TB/1042; Vol. II, TB/1043
W. A. Dunning	RECONSTRUCTION, POLITICAL AND ECONOMIC TB/1073
George Eliot	DANIEL DERONDA. A novel. Introduction by F. R. Leavis TB/1039
John N. Figgis	POLITICAL THOUGHT FROM GERSON TO GROTIUS: 1414–1625: *Seven Studies.* Introduction by Garrett Mattingly TB/1032
Editors of *Fortune*	AMERICA IN THE SIXTIES: *The Economy and the Society* TB/1015
F. L. Ganshof	FEUDALISM TB/1058
G. P. Gooch	ENGLISH DEMOCRATIC IDEAS IN THE SEVENTEENTH CENTURY TB/1006
Albert Goodwin	THE FRENCH REVOLUTION TB/1064
Francis J. Grund	ARISTOCRACY IN AMERICA: *A Study of Jacksonian Democracy* TB/1001
W. K. C. Guthrie	THE GREEK PHILOSOPHERS: *From Thales to Aristotle* TB/1008
Marcus Lee Hansen	THE ATLANTIC MIGRATION: 1607–1860. Intro. by Oscar Handlin TB/1052
Alfred Harbage	AS THEY LIKED IT: *A Study of Shakespeare's Moral Artistry* TB/1035
John Higham, *Ed.*	THE RECONSTRUCTION OF AMERICAN HISTORY TB/1068
J. M. Hussey	THE BYZANTINE WORLD TB/1057
Dan N. Jacobs, *Ed.*	THE NEW COMMUNIST MANIFESTO TB/1078
Henry James	THE PRINCESS CASAMASSIMA. A novel. Intro. by Clinton Oliver TB/1005
Henry James	RODERICK HUDSON. A novel. Introduction by Leon Edel TB/1016
Henry James	THE TRAGIC MUSE. A novel. Introduction by Leon Edel TB/1017
William James	PSYCHOLOGY: *The Briefer Course.* Ed. with Intro. by G. Allport TB/1034
Arnold Kettle	AN INTRODUCTION TO THE ENGLISH NOVEL. Vol. I, *Defoe to George Eliot,* TB/1011; Vol. II, *Henry James to the Present.* TB/1012
Hans Kohn, *Ed.*	THE MIND OF MODERN RUSSIA: *Historical and Political Thought* TB/1065
Samuel Noah Kramer	SUMERIAN MYTHOLOGY: *A Study of Spiritual and Literary Achievement in the Third Millennium B.C.* Illustrated TB/1055
Paul Oskar Kristeller	RENAISSANCE THOUGHT: *Classic, Scholastic, Humanist Strains* TB/1048
L. S. B. Leakey	ADAM'S ANCESTORS: *The Evolution of Man and His Culture.* TB/1019
Bernard Lewis	THE ARABS IN HISTORY TB/1029
Ferdinand Lot	THE END OF THE ANCIENT WORLD AND THE BEGINNINGS OF THE MIDDLE AGES. Introduction by Glanville Downey TB/1044
Arthur O. Lovejoy	THE GREAT CHAIN OF BEING: *A Study of the History of an Idea* TB/1009
Robert Lowie	PRIMITIVE SOCIETY. Introduction by Fred Eggan TB/1056
Niccolo Machiavelli	HISTORY OF FLORENCE AND OF THE AFFAIRS OF ITALY: *From Earliest Times to Death of Lorenzo the Magnificent.* Intro. by F. Gilbert TB/1027
J. P. Mayer	ALEXIS DE TOCQUEVILLE: *A Biographical Study in Political Science* TB/1014

HARPER TORCHBOOKS / The Bollingen Library

HARPER TORCHBOOKS / The Cloister Library

HARPER TORCHBOOKS / The Science Library